KV-193-611

FRUIT
for all seasons

COMPILED BY JENNENE PLUMMER

PHOTOGRAPHY BY
QUENTIN BACON AND ASHLEY BARBER

BayBooks
An imprint of HarperCollins*Publishers*

ACKNOWLEDGEMENTS
The publishers would like to thank the following people and organisations
for their assistance during the production of this book:

Sue Dodd and the Sydney Market Authority for the following recipes:
Blueberry and Goat's Cheese Salad
Berry Flan
Ruby Clafoutis
Passionfruit Sauce
Banana Soufflé
and for the transparency reproduced on page 41

Yvonne Webb for the following recipes:
Fish Shashlik
Lemon Sorbet
Fruit-filled Dumplings

Sherringhams Nursery, North Ryde, for fruit trees

Designer: Leonie Bremer-Kamp
Design Assistant: Russell Jeffery
Food Editor: Jennene Plummer
Editorial Assistant: Suzanna Norton

A BAY BOOKS PUBLICATION
An imprint of HarperCollinsPublishers

First published in Australia in 1992 by
CollinsAngus&Robertson Publishers Pty Limited (ACN 009 913 517)
A division of HarperCollinsPublishers (Australia) Pty Limited
25-31 Ryde Road, Pymble NSW 2073, Australia

HarperCollinsPublishers (New Zealand) Limited
31 View Road, Glenfield, Auckland 10, New Zealand

HarperCollinsPublishers Limited
77-85 Fulham Palace Road, London W6 8JB, United Kingdom

Copyright © Bay Books 1992

This book is copyright.
Apart from any fair dealing for the purposes of private study,
research, criticism or review, as permitted under the Copyright
Act, no part may be reproduced by any process without written
permission. Inquiries should be addressed to the publishers.

ISBN 186 378 0033

Cover and chapter opening photography by Quentin Bacon,
with stylist Jennene Plummer
Printed in Singapore

5 4 3 2 1
96 95 94 93 92

Contents

Apples and Pears 6

Citrus Fruits 18

Berries 34

Stone Fruits 42

Fruits from the Vine 54

Melons 64

Fresh from the Tropics 72

PICK OF THE CROP 90

MEASURING MADE EASY 94

INDEX 95

FRUIT FOR ALL SEASONS

For snacks, starters, main meals and great finishes, fruit is the answer. It's delicious, it's easy to prepare, it's full of vitamins and minerals and it's so good. A platter piled high with fresh fruits is undoubtedly one of the most refreshing, and simple ways to end a meal.

NATURE'S BOUNTY

Since classic times, the symbol of abundance has been the cornucopia – a horn of plenty overflowing with ripened fruit. *Fruit for All Seasons* brings you an abundance of tantalising recipes using nature's fabulous bounty.

FRUIT FOR HEALTH

With people becoming more and more health conscious, fruit is a definite asset in today's fresh food revolution that is quietly changing our eating patterns.

FRUIT FOR VARIETY

Many people think that fruit only belongs in desserts, jams and punches – now they can think again. Fruit can add a tangy vibrancy and melt-in-the-mouth texture to all sorts of savoury dishes.

The range of fruit available to us today seems limitless. From the exotic and unusual to the more familiar, fruit is an abundant source of great taste and good nutrition.

Whether it comes to us from trees, vines or bushes, fruit can be served with little or no preparation; however, with just a little imagination, you can transform it into a feast of culinary delights.

Within a meal, fruit is traditionally served as a dessert or a refreshing starter, but it need not be limited to these roles. Fruit sauces complement meat, poultry and even fish dishes beautifully. Fruit

combined with salad ingredients adds a special tang. Fruit and cheese is a simply delicious way to end a meal – whether casual or formal. And for an added touch, why not dip a few strawberries in a little melted chocolate!

And, let's not forget the delights of homemade jams and chutneys or fresh fruit shakes.

FRUIT BOWLS

Fruit's versatility extends beyond cooking. Scoop the contents out of fruits such as grapefuit, rockmelon (cantaloupe) large oranges, pineapple, watermelon and avocado to create fruit shell serving dishes.

FRUIT'S TENDER TOUCH

Fruit is also a natural tenderiser. Wrap pawpaw leaves around meat or octopus overnight or marinate meats in pawpaw juice or the juice of kiwi fruit – they are the ideal natural tenderisers.

FRUITFUL TIPS

This book is filled with hints and tips to help make preparing these simple recipes even easier (including how to choose and store the various fruits). There are also notes on the best times to buy in our Pick of the Crop chart at the end of the book.

FRUIT DELIGHTS

We know the recipes in our book will inspire you to create your own fresh and innovative combinations, or to experiment with the new, exotic, more unfamiliar fruits now available.

Whatever your choice, fruit will delight your eye and palate throughout the year – spring, summer, autumn and winter. It is truly fine fare for all seasons.

APPLES *and* PEARS

Apples are, without doubt, one of the most popular fruits. Thanks to cultivation over the years, there are now over 3000 known varieties. Whether green, red or yellow, their fresh flavour and crisp texture are unmistakable and appetising on just about any occasion.

Cooking apples are normally green and cook down well to a purée. Try apples in salads, pies, tarts, baked, fried as an accompaniment to meat (especially pork or game) or made into fritters. Look for apples with tight, smooth, unmarked skin. Avoid those with bruises or cuts. Apples keep very well.

Pears come in many different shapes and sizes and are equally delicious whether firm or juicy ripe. Pears ripen very quickly, so buy while still firm and allow them to ripen in a cool, dark place. Keep pears refrigerated if you want them to last longer. Pears are popular poached, wrapped in pastry, in salads, with cheese, in soufflés, sorbets and jams.

Recipes in this section cover ideas from soups through to cakes and preserves. We have also included recipes using Nashi pears as well as figs.

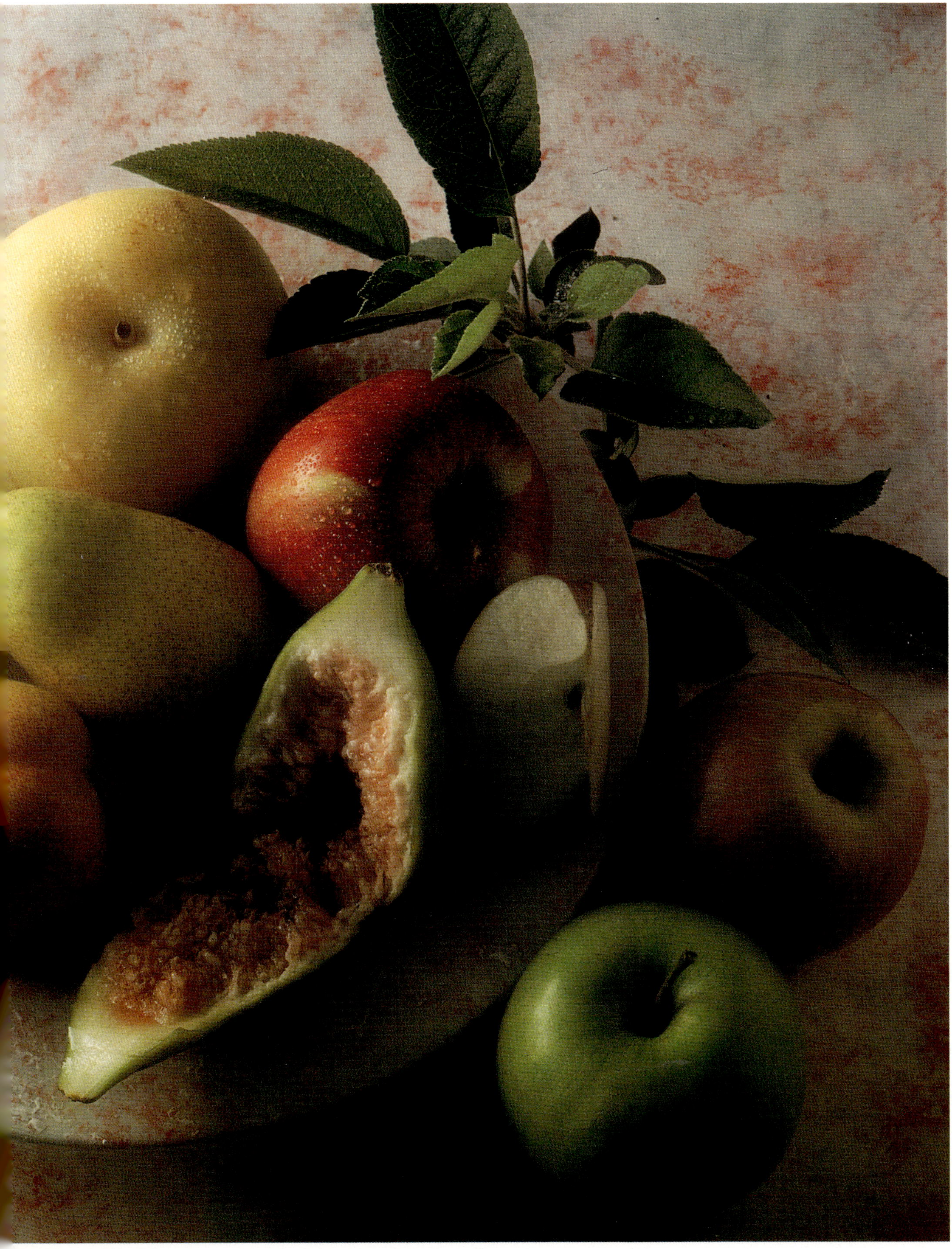

STEWING FRUIT

When stewing fruit use minimal water. Berries, rhubarb and juicy fruits need only a few tablespoons, while other fruit (such as apples) should be half covered. To maintain shape of fruit when stewing, always boil sugar and water together first before adding the fruit. Simmer gently until tender.

TO SAUTÉ

Sauté is a quick cooking method meaning to toss food in a pan over high heat.

CHILLED PEAR *and* LIME SOUP

1 cup (250 g) caster sugar

4 cups (1 litre) water or pear nectar

4 pears peeled, cored and puréed

juice 6 limes

1 cup (250 ml) white wine

2 tablespoons lime zest

300 ml sour cream

1 Place sugar and water in a 2 litre saucepan. Over a low heat, stir until sugar is dissolved. Bring to boil. Reduce heat and simmer for 5 minutes.

2 Add puréed pears, lime juice and white wine. Simmer for further 10 minutes.

3 Remove from heat. Set aside to cool. Stir in lime zest and sour cream. Transfer to soup tureen or bowl. Chill and serve.

SERVES 8

CURRIED CHICKEN SOUP

30 g butter or ghee

1 large onion, peeled and sliced

2 celery stalks with green tops, sliced

3 tablespoons plain flour

1 tablespoon curry powder

2 large green apples, roughly chopped

250 g cooked chicken meat, chopped

5 cups (1.25 litres) chicken stock

1 tablespoon lemon juice

salt and pepper, to taste

GARNISH

natural yoghurt or thickened cream

chopped fresh chives

1 Melt butter in a large pan. Sauté onion and celery for about 5 minutes until softened. Add flour and curry powder and continue cooking for 3 minutes, stirring occasionally to prevent sticking.

2 Stir in apple, chicken and 1 cup (250 ml) of stock. Simmer for about 5 minutes. Cool slightly.

3 Purée mixture in a food processor or blender. This may need to be done in several batches. Return purée to pan. Add the remaining chicken stock, lemon juice and seasonings.

4 Bring to boil. Simmer for about 10 minutes, cool, cover and chill in refrigerator. Serve cold with a spoonful of yoghurt or cream in each bowl and a sprinkle of chopped chives.

SERVES 4

Curried Chicken Soup

RED CABBAGE *and* APPLE

30 g butter or margarine

1 medium-sized red cabbage, finely shredded

2 tablespoons honey

1 small onion, peeled and grated

1 apple, grated

1 pear, peeled and chopped

¼ cup (60 ml) red wine

2 tablespoons lemon juice

1 Melt butter in a large pan and sauté the cabbage with the honey. Add the onion, apple, pear, wine and lemon juice. Bring to the boil.

2 Simmer, covered, for 1 hour, shaking pan occasionally during cooking.

SERVES 6 TO 8

APPLE *and* DATE SALAD *with* CALIFORNIAN SALAD DRESSING

3 crisp apples, cored and chopped to make 4 cups

1 cup (100 g) stoned, chopped fresh dates

½ cup (60 g) slivered almonds

4 firm lettuce leaves

CALIFORNIAN SALAD DRESSING

1 tablespoon Worcestershire sauce

1 tablespoon olive oil

1 teaspoon lemon juice

grated rind ½ lemon

1 Mix apples, dates and almonds together with dressing. Pile in lettuce leaf cups.

2 TO PREPARE CALIFORNIAN SALAD DRESSING: Combine ingredients together in screwtop jar and shake well.

SERVES 4

PREPARING APPLES

When apples and pears are cut they turn brown due to oxidation. To prevent this, toss them in lemon juice.

Always core apples before you peel them if you want them to stay whole. They tend to collapse if cored after peeling.

Apple and Date Salad with Californian Salad Dressing

Mulligatawny

MULLIGATAWNY

Serve with a bowl of hot boiled rice, Indian or pita bread. This spicy soup can also be made from beef, mutton or fish.

MULLIGATAWNY

750 g chicken pieces

4 cups (1 litre) chicken stock

1 onion, peeled and sliced

1 carrot, peeled and sliced

1 stalk celery, sliced

30 g butter or margarine

2 onions, peeled and finely chopped

2 green apples, peeled, cored and sliced

2 tablespoons plain flour

1 tablespoon curry powder

1 bay leaf

¼ teaspoon allspice

4 tablespoons cream

1 Place chicken pieces in a casserole. Add stock, onion, carrot and celery. Cover. Simmer for 1 hour.

2 Remove chicken pieces. Discard skin and bones. Cut chicken meat into small pieces.

3 Strain stock. Chill for 4 hours then remove fat from surface.

4 Melt butter in a saucepan. Sauté onions and apples together for 3 minutes. Stir in flour and curry powder. Cook 1 minute.

5 Add stock, bay leaf and allspice. Cover and simmer 15 minutes. Blend in chicken and cream. Continue cooking for 5 minutes until chicken is hot.

SERVES 8

CORIANDER *and* PEAR SALAD

The flavour of coriander and pear is delightful. A few pecan or walnuts may be added to give this salad extra crunch.

4 ripe Nashi pears

1 bunch watercress

200 g pear or cherry tomatoes

6 tablespoons chopped fresh coriander leaves

½ bunch spring onions, slivered

½ bunch chives, snipped

DRESSING

½ cup (125 ml) olive oil

2 to 3 tablespoons lemon juice

2 teaspoons Dijon-style mustard

1 clove garlic, peeled and crushed with a pinch salt

freshly ground black pepper

1 Peel, halve and core pears. Slice lengthways. Arrange in a salad bowl lined with watercress. Scatter over tomatoes, coriander, spring onions and chives.

2 TO PREPARE DRESSING: Place all ingredients in a small bowl. Whisk together until combined. Pour over salad. Lightly toss just before serving.

SERVES 4

LAMB CURRY

Serve this curry with boiled rice, garnished with red capsicum (pepper) or lemon.

1¼ kg boned shoulder or leg of lamb, trimmed and cubed

½ cup (60 g) plain flour

salt and freshly ground black pepper to taste

90 g butter or margarine

2 green apples, peeled, cored and sliced

2 onions, peeled and chopped

1 tomato, quartered

2 cloves garlic, crushed

1 to 2 tablespoons curry powder

1¾ cups (435 ml) stock or water

2 tablespoons sultanas or raisins

2 tablespoons desiccated coconut

1 teaspoon brown sugar

grated rind and juice of ½ lemon

1 tablespoon flaked almonds

1 Toss meat in combined flour and seasonings. Shake off excess.

2 Melt butter in a large pan. Add meat. Brown well. Remove from pan and set aside.

3 Add apples, onions, tomato, garlic and curry powder to pan. Cook for 2 to 3 minutes. Pour off any excess fat.

4 Stir stock into pan with all remaining ingredients except almonds. Return meat to pan. Simmer, covered, for 2 hours or until meat is tender. Stir in almonds.

SERVES 6

APPLE TIPS

Apples look attractive if presented cored and cut into rings or quartered, cored and sliced.

Apple skins provide lovely colour, so leave them on unless told otherwise in the recipe.

PEAR TIPS

Pear flesh is extremely delicate, so handle with care.

If whole pears are required, core by working an apple corer in from the base or use a small spoon.

QUAIL *with* WILD RICE *and* APPLE

9 quail (1½ quail per serve)

8 juniper berries marinated 2 to 3 hours in 3 tablespoons Madeira

1½ cups (375 ml) chicken stock

STUFFING

30 g butter or margarine

2 spring onions, finely chopped

liver and heart of quail, diced

1½ cups wild rice, cooked

1 large red apple, cored and diced

2 tablespoons cream

1 egg yolk

salt and pepper to taste

pinch lemon thyme

MIREPOIX

30 g butter or margarine

2 spring onions, chopped

1 small carrot diced

1 small stick celery diced

TO REDUCE

Reduce means to boil or rapidly simmer a mixture until evaporation occurs and the mixture thickens.

MIREPOIX

A mirepoix is a mixture of sautéed mixed vegetables used in meat, fish and shellfish dishes to enhance flavour.

1 With quails on their backs and starting at the tail end, make an incision along breast. Carefully remove all small bones from breast and back sections, leaving the legs intact.

2 TO PREPARE STUFFING: Melt butter in a pan. Add spring onions. Cook until softened. Add the liver and heart of quail. Cook 5 minutes. Mix in the wild rice and diced apple. Bind all ingredients together with cream and egg yolk. Season to taste.

3 TO PREPARE MIREPOIX: Melt butter. Sauté vegetables until tender. Spoon into the base of an ovenproof dish.

4 Spoon stuffing into cavity of quails. Stitch incision with cotton. Arrange quails over mirepoix in one layer. Bake at 200°C (400°F) for 15 to 20 minutes, basting frequently. Lift quails from dish and remove stitches. Keep warm.

5 TO PREPARE SAUCE: Discard vegetables, but pour pan juices into a small saucepan. Add juniper berry mixture and chicken stock. Bring sauce to boil. Reduce until thickened. Season, strain and spoon the sauce over the quails before serving.

SERVES 6

PEAR PROSCIUTTO

250 g prosciutto, thinly sliced

4 pears, peeled and sliced

2 kiwi fruit, peeled and sliced

1 mango, peeled, seeded and sliced

GARNISH

creamed cottage cheese

1 Arrange slices of prosciutto and fruits alternately on a large serving platter or 4 individual plates. Serve with creamed cottage cheese.

SERVES 4

Quail with Wild Rice and Apple

Apple Strudel

10 sheets filo pastry

125 g butter or margarine, melted

1 cup (60 g) fresh breadcrumbs

4 apples, peeled, cored and chopped

⅔ cup (125 g) raisins

½ cup (60 g) chopped walnuts

1 teaspoon cinnamon or mixed spice

3 to 4 tablespoons rum or grated rind and juice 1 lemon

½ cup (125 g) caster sugar

2 tablespoons milk

¼ cup (45 g) icing sugar

1 Brush 5 sheets of filo pastry with melted butter, placing one on top of the other. Set aside. Repeat with remaining pastry sheets. Set aside separately, covered with damp tea towel.

2 Scatter breadcrumbs over first layer of pastry. Spread with combined apple, raisins, chopped walnuts and spices. Sprinkle with rum and sugar.

3 Place second layer of pastry over the fruit. Roll strudel up. Place on greased baking sheet. Brush top with milk.

4 Bake at 200°C (400°F) for 30 minutes. Place on serving dish and dust with icing sugar. Cut into slices. Serve warm.

SERVES 8 TO 10

Apple Spice Cake

500 g Granny Smith apples, peeled, cored, and sliced

4 tablespoons water

juice ½ lemon

180 g butter or margarine

½ cup (90 g) brown sugar

3½ cups (450 g) wholemeal flour

1 teaspoon bicarbonate of soda

1 teaspoon ground cinnamon

½ teaspoon ground nutmeg

½ teaspoon ground mace

¼ teaspoon ground cloves

1 cup (180 g) chopped walnuts

1 cup (180 g) chopped dates

⅓ cup (60 g) raisins

3 tablespoons milk

TOPPING

1 tablespoon brown sugar

¼ cup (30 g) chopped walnuts

½ teaspoon cinnamon

Apple Strudel

1 Cook apples over low heat in water and lemon juice until soft. Mash with wooden spoon. Leave to cool.

2 Cream butter and sugar until light and fluffy. Sift flour with bicarbonate of soda and spices into creamed mixture. Blend in with walnuts, dates, raisins, apple and milk. Spoon into greased 12 cm x 34 cm loaf pan.

3 TO PREPARE TOPPING: Combine topping ingredients. Sprinkle over cake. Bake at 180°C (350°F) for 1¼ to 1½ hours. Leave to rest in pan for 15 minutes. Turn out onto a wire rack to cool.

SIFTING FLOUR

When sifting wholegrain flours, tip any leftover grains into mixture, don't throw them away.

Pear Tart with Frangipani Cream

200°C (400 F) for 10 minutes. Cool before filling.

2 Cook pears in water, sugar and lemon rind until just tender. Cool in syrup. Drain on paper towel.

3 TO PREPARE FRANGIPANI CREAM: Cream butter and sugar together. Add eggs a little at a time, beating well. Combine almonds, flour and kirsch. Blend into a creamed mixture.

4 Spoon half the Frangipani Cream over pastry base. Arrange pear halves on this, cut-side facing down. Spread the remaining cream mixture around and over the pears.

5 Bake at 180°C (350°F) for 40 minutes or until cream is set and golden-brown on top. Brush with apricot jam.

SERVES 8

APPLE *and* PLUM CRUMBLE

500 g cooking apples, peeled, cored and sliced

500 g plums, halved and stoned

1 cup (250 g) caster sugar

3 to 4 tablespoons orange juice

125 g butter or margarine, cubed

2¼ cups (280 g) plain flour, sifted

½ cup (60 g) flaked almonds

grated rind 1 orange

1 Place half the fruit in a large, ovenproof dish. Sprinkle over ¼ cup (60 g) sugar and the orange juice before placing remaining fruit in dish.

2 Rub butter into flour until mixture resembles fine breadcrumbs. Stir in remaining sugar, almonds and orange rind.

3 Spread crumble mixture thickly over fruit. Bake at 180°C (350°F) for 35 to 40 minutes or until top is slightly golden. Serve immediately, with whipped cream or custard.

SERVES 6 TO 8

TO BAKE BLIND

Cover pastry with baking paper and dried beans or uncooked rice. Bake at 200°C (400°F) for 5 minutes. Remove baking paper and beans. Bake further 5 minutes. Allow to cool.

PEAR TART *with* FRANGIPANI CREAM

2 sheets ready-rolled shortcrust pastry

4 pears, peeled, halved and cored

2 cups (500 ml) water

1 cup (250 g) sugar

strip of lemon rind

¾ cup (300 g) apricot jam, warmed and sieved

FRANGIPANI CREAM

125 g unsalted butter or margarine

½ cup (125 g) sugar

2 large eggs, beaten

1 cup (250 g) ground almonds

1 tablespoon plain flour

a few drops of kirsch or almond essence

1 Line base and sides of a 25 cm flan dish with pastry. Trim edges. Bake blind at

STEP-BY-STEP TECHNIQUES

BAKED PEAR SURPRISE

Leave stalks on peeled pears for a very attractive effect. This recipe can be used with other fruits such as apples and peaches. Or you can serve a variety of fruits prepared this way.

125 g butter or margarine

3 to 4 tablespoons sugar

3 to 4 tablespoons ground almonds

pinch cinnamon

1 egg, separated

1 tablespoon orange liqueur

4 eating pears, ripe and tender

500 g readymade puff pastry

2 tablespoons apricot jam

1 Make a stiff paste by creaming butter, sugar, ground almonds and cinnamon together. Gradually add egg yolk. Stir in orange liqueur.

2 Peel and core pears. Split in half. Fill centres with paste. Press the two halves together.

3 Roll out puff pastry into 4 oblong pieces, 10 cm x 20 cm. Place a pear in the middle of each. Brush edges with water. Fold oblong to enclose each pear, retaining the pear shape. Make two small cuts at the top to allow steam to escape. Brush with egg white. Rest for 15 minutes.

4 Place on greased baking trays. Bake at 200°C (400°F) for 20 minutes.

5 Heat apricot jam until liquid. Strain. When pears are taken from oven, brush them lightly with hot jam as a glaze. Serve hot with ice cream or custard.

SERVES 4

Cream butter, sugar, cinnamon and almonds

Peel and core pears, split in half and fill centres

Enclose pear in pastry, retaining pear shape

Apple Almond Flan

Pastry

1½ cups (180 g) plain flour

90 g butter or margarine, cubed

1 egg yolk

1 to 2 tablespoons lemon juice or water

Filling

125 g butter or margarine

½ cup (125 g) caster sugar

2 eggs

60 g ground almonds

1 tablespoon plain flour

3 green apples, peeled, cored and thinly sliced

2 tablespoons sieved apricot jam (optional)

icing sugar for dusting

1   To Prepare Pastry: Sift flour into a bowl. Rub in butter or margarine using fingertips, until the mixture resembles breadcrumbs.

2   Mix in egg yolk, and enough lemon juice to make a soft, pliable dough. Wrap in plastic wrap and rest in refrigerator for at least 20 minutes.

3   To Prepare Filling: Cream butter and sugar together until light and creamy. Beat in eggs, almonds and flour and set aside.

4   Roll out pastry to fit a greased 23 cm flan tin. Trim edges. Refrigerate for 10 to 15 minutes.

5   Spread almond filling over pastry base. Smooth top.

6   Arrange apple slices decoratively over the filling, pressing in lightly.

7   Bake in a moderately hot oven at 190°C (375°F) for 15 minutes. Reduce temperature to 180°C (350°F) and bake for a further 25 to 30 minutes or until set and golden.

8   Heat jam gently. Brush over apples. Cool and serve dusted with icing sugar.

Serves 8 to 10

Apple Almond Flan

FRESH FIG *and* APPLE JAM

500 g fresh figs, washed and sliced

2 cooking apples (about 250 g), peeled, cored and sliced

juice 3 lemons

grated rind 1 lemon

2 cups (500 g) sugar

1 Place figs and apples in preserving pan with lemon juice and lemon rind. Cover and cook gently over low heat.

2 When fruit is very soft, add sugar. Stir until dissolved. Bring to the boil. Boil rapidly until setting point is reached or until temperature on sugar thermometer is 105°C (210°F).

3 Spoon jam into hot clean jars, cover with waxed paper discs and seal.

MAKES ABOUT 1 KG

APPLE BUTTER

750 g cooking apples

2½ cups (625 ml) cider

caster sugar as needed

½ teaspoon ground cinnamon

½ teaspoon ground cloves

grated rind ½ lemon

1 Wash, quarter and core apples, but do not remove skins. Place in large pan with cider. Bring to the boil. Simmer gently until apples turn pulpy.

2 Pass apples and cider through a sieve. Discard residue. Measure quantity of fruit purée and add 1½ cups (325 g) caster sugar to each 2½ cups (625 ml) purée. Return purée and sugar to pan.

3 Add spices and lemon rind. Stir purée over low heat until sugar dissolves. Stir constantly until mixture is very thick, creamy and almost solid.

4 Place in heated, sterilised jars. Seal and cool.

MAKES ABOUT 1.5 KG

APPLE *and* PEAR MUSTARD

1 cup (250 ml) dry white wine

½ cup (125 ml) white grape juice

2 sticks cinnamon

pared rind 1 lemon

375 g green cooking apples, peeled, cored and diced

375 g pears, peeled, cored and diced

small bunch (150 g) seedless white grapes, peeled

200 g Dijon mustard

½ teaspoon dark mustard seeds

1 Place wine, grape juice, cinnamon sticks and lemon rind in a saucepan. Bring to the boil. Simmer for 5 minutes.

2 Discard lemon rind. Simmer for a further 5 minutes. Discard cinnamon sticks.

3 Add fruit. Simmer for 15 to 20 minutes or until just tender. Carefully blend in mustard and seeds. Simmer for a further 2 to 3 minutes. Pour into warm, sterilised jars. Seal.

MAKES 3½ CUPS.

SETTING JAM

The setting point for jams and marmalades is best measured on a sugar thermometer. If you don't have a sugar thermometer, to test if set, place a little marmalade on a cool plate. If the skin forms wrinkles when pushed with a finger, the marmalade is set.

CITRUS

Oranges, lemons, limes, grapefruit, pomelo, mandarins, tangerines and cumquats all belong to the citrus family. They span a spectrum of flavours from sharp and bitter to sweet and tangy, each enhancing cookery in very special ways.

Choose firm, bright, glossy, unblemished fruit with no soft spots. Store in a cool place. As the skin of a mandarin is loose, they do not keep as well as tight-skinned oranges. If fruit has been cut, cover with plastic wrap, store in the refrigerator and use within a few days. Citrus fruit will keep in the refrigerator for several weeks.

Lemons and limes are traditional accompaniments to fish and seafood but also make wonderful desserts. Oranges are often included in salads and are used in many different desserts.

Our recipes cover ideas from soups, dressings and main meals to sweets and preserves. Their usage in cooking is almost endless.

CARROT and ORANGE SOUP

750 g carrots, peeled and sliced

1 onion, peeled and chopped

2 sticks celery, chopped

4 cups (1 litre) chicken or vegetable stock

1 bay leaf

1 tablespoon cornflour

grated rind and juice of 1 orange

good pinch nutmeg

seasoning to taste

3 to 4 tablespoons cream (optional)

1 Place vegetables in a pan with the stock and bay leaf. Cover and simmer for 20 minutes, until the vegetables are tender. Purée vegetables in food processor or push through a sieve.

2 Blend cornflour with a little of the soup.

3 Return the puréed vegetables to the soup with the blended cornflour, orange rind and juice, nutmeg and seasonings. Bring to the boil. Simmer for 3 minutes, stirring.

4 Pour soup into a serving bowl. Decorate with a swirl of cream.

SERVES 6

TABBOULEH

Chop parsley and mint in a food processor for added convenience.

¾ cup (180 g) burghul (cracked wheat)

1½ bunches Italian parsley, finely chopped

½ bunch spring onions, finely chopped

6 tablespoons finely chopped fresh mint

juice 1 large lemon

3 to 4 tablespoons olive oil

2 tomatoes, roughly chopped

salt and freshly ground black pepper

1 Soak burghul in water to cover for 10 minutes or until all water is absorbed.

2 Place burghul in a salad bowl with parsley, spring onions and mint. Pour over lemon juice and oil. Lightly fork through tomato and seasonings.

SERVES 4 TO 6

CITRUS and MANGO SALAD with CREAM DRESSING

1 lettuce, leaves washed and dried

3 stalks celery, cut into 8 cm pieces

425 g can mango slices, drained

3 oranges, peeled and segmented

1 cucumber, scored and finely sliced

6 spring onions, finely sliced

CREAM DRESSING

4 tablespoons mayonnaise

½ cup (125 ml) cream

salt and freshly ground black pepper

2 tablespoons chopped parsley

1 teaspoon French mustard

3 teaspoons orange juice

2 teaspoons lemon juice

1 Arrange lettuce leaves on a serving plate.

2 Make celery curls by slicing the celery lengthways leaving one end uncut. Drop celery into iced water until it curls.

3 Arrange mango slices, orange segments, celery curls and cucumber between lettuce leaves. Garnish with spring onions. Refrigerate until ready to serve.

4 TO MAKE DRESSING: Combine all ingredients. Stand for 15 to 20 minutes before using. Serve separately.

SERVES 6 TO 8

FRUITED CHICKEN SALAD

1½ to 2 cups (300 g) cooked, diced chicken meat

½ cup (60 g) cooked brown long grain rice

2 grapefruit, peeled and segmented

2 carrots, cut into julienne strips

2 teaspoons chopped onion

1 large ripe avocado

2 tablespoons lemon juice

1 tablespoon vinegar

1 tablespoon oil

lettuce leaves for serving

watercress, to garnish

DRESSING

6 tablespoons mayonnaise

1 teaspoon curry powder

1 Place chicken, rice, grapefruit, carrots and onion into a salad bowl and toss well.

2 Peel and dice avocado. Brush with lemon juice.

3 Combine vinegar and oil. Add to chicken mixture with avocado and lemon juice and toss gently.

5 Serve salad on bed of lettuce. Garnish with watercress.

6 TO MAKE DRESSING: Combine all ingredients. Serve dressing separately.

SERVES 4

Fruited Chicken Salad

Arrange salad ingredients, marinate avocado

Combine oil and vinegar and add to salad

Blend salad dressing ingredients together

Florida Salad with Walnut Mayonnaise

BROCCOLI SALAD *with* LIME MAYONNAISE

This tangy salad is served sprinkled with Italian Dressing and accompanied by Lime Mayonnaise.

3 large heads broccoli, cut into florets

ITALIAN DRESSING
2 tablespoons wine vinegar
½ clove garlic, peeled and crushed
salt and freshly ground black pepper
1 cup (250 ml) olive oil
1 tablespoon finely chopped fresh parsley

LIME MAYONNAISE
2 cups (500 ml) mayonnaise
2 cups (500 ml) light sour cream
⅓ cup (80 ml) freshly squeezed lime juice
1 tablespoon finely grated lime peel
2 tablespoons grated horseradish root
1 tablespoon Dijon-style mustard

1 Place florets in a steamer. Steam over boiling water until just tender (approximately 3 minutes). If you have only a small steamer this can be done in batches.
2 When cooked, plunge instantly into iced water, taking care not to break the florets. Cool. Cover with plastic wrap. Refrigerate overnight.
3 TO PREPARE ITALIAN DRESSING: Combine vinegar, garlic, salt and pepper. Gradually whisk in oil and parsley. Sprinkle over broccoli florets just before serving.
4 TO PREPARE LIME MAYONNAISE: Whisk ingredients together in a bowl. This dressing can be prepared in advance and stored in the refrigerator. Serve separately.

SERVES 8 TO 10

CITRUS SEGMENTS

To segment citrus fruit (this is usually for oranges), peel all the skin and the white pith away. Cut down between the membranes with a very sharp knife and remove segments.

FLORIDA SALAD *with* WALNUT MAYONNAISE

3 tomatoes, diced
2 apples, diced
2 oranges, peeled and segmented
1 grapefruit, peeled and segmented
3 tablespoons mayonnaise
1 tablespoon sugar
1 tablespoon cream cheese
1 tablespoon chopped walnuts
lettuce leaves to serve

1 Combine tomatoes, apples, oranges and grapefruit in a bowl.
2 Blend or process mayonnaise, sugar, cream cheese and walnuts together. Pour over the salad ingredients. Toss well. Cover and chill thoroughly before serving.
3 Serve on a bed of lettuce. Mayonnaise may be served separately.

SERVES 4 TO 6

LEMON YOGHURT DRESSING

An oil-free dressing made with fresh herbs that is ideal for pawpaw, grapes, melons and strawberries.

⅔ cup (160 ml) yoghurt
1 tablespoon finely chopped parsley
1 tablespoon finely chopped chives
1 tablespoon finely chopped thyme or mint
finely grated rind and juice ½ lemon
freshly ground black pepper

1 Combine all ingredients in a screwtop jar. Shake to mix well. Refrigerate until required.

MAKES ⅔ CUP (160 ML)

AIOLI

This delicious garlic mayonnaise goes particularly well with fresh seafood.

12 to 16 cloves garlic, peeled and coarsely chopped
3 egg yolks
salt and freshly ground black pepper
2 cups (500 ml) olive oil
juice 2 lemons

1 Purée garlic and egg yolks in a food processor or blender. Add salt and pepper.
2 With motor still running, add oil in a thin stream, slowly at first. As the sauce thickens, add lemon juice.
3 Taste, adding a little more lemon juice, salt or pepper if necessary.

MAKES 2½ CUPS (625 ML)

LEMON GRASS CHICKEN

Before using the shrimp paste, wrap the amount required in a small piece of aluminium foil and roast in a dry frying pan for a few minutes. Cool and use as required.

4 stalks lemon grass, thinly sliced
½ bunch spring onions, chopped
1 onion, peeled and chopped
1 teaspoon shrimp paste
1½ cups (375 ml) coconut milk
1 tablespoon raw sugar
1 tablespoon curry powder
1 kg chicken pieces, skin removed
juice 1 lemon
4 tablespoons oil
2 tablespoons sambal oelek (chopped chilli)
½ cup (125 ml) water
2 lime leaves or ½ teaspoon lime peel
salt and freshly ground black pepper, to taste

1 Place lemon grass, spring onions, onion, shrimp paste and ½ cup (125 ml) coconut milk in a food processor. Process to make a fine paste.
2 Mix sugar and curry powder together in a small bowl. Rub chicken pieces with lemon juice. Spread curry mixture over chicken. Allow to marinate for about 1 hour.
3 Heat oil in a heavy flameproof casserole. Add sambal oelek. Cook, stirring, for 1 minute.
4 Add chicken. Fry until golden brown. Add lemon grass mixture, the remaining coconut milk, water, lime leaves and seasonings. Simmer uncovered for 35 minutes or until chicken is tender and sauce thickens slightly. Serve with steamed rice.

SERVES 4 TO 6

ZEST

The outer layer of citrus fruit skin is known as zest. It may be removed by using a grater (ensure only the colour of the skin is removed, as the white pith underneath is bitter) or may be peeled off using a vegetable peeler. These pieces of skin may be sliced thinly, blanched and used in recipes. A zester will make even finer strips, and this peel does not require blanching.

LEMONS AS GARNISH

Lemons make wonderful garnishes for many dishes either sliced, twisted, cut into wedges and so on.

GREMOLATA

The lemon, garlic and parsley gremolata makes this ossobuco something special.

OSSOBUCO ALLA MILANESE

8 pieces veal shank

plain flour

90 g butter or margarine

1 small onion, peeled and thinly sliced

1 small carrot, scrubbed and sliced

1 small piece celery, sliced

1 clove garlic, peeled and sliced

salt and freshly ground black pepper

½ cup (125 ml) white wine

425 g can tomatoes

1 cup (250 ml) beef stock

GREMOLATA

4 tablespoons chopped fresh parsley

1 clove garlic, peeled and finely chopped

grated zest 1 lemon

1 Dust veal in flour. Melt butter in a pan and brown the veal well.

2 Add the onion, carrot, celery, garlic and seasonings. Stir and turn veal occasionally.

3 When everything in the pan has acquired a lovely golden colour, add wine. Simmer until liquid has almost completely evaporated.

4 Add the sieved tomatoes and stock. Cook slowly for just over an hour or until the meat is so tender it falls easily from the bone. If the sauce becomes too thick, add a few tablespoons of water.

5 TO PREPARE GREMOLATA: Combine parsley, garlic and grated lemon. Serve ossobuco sprinkled with gremolata.

SERVES 4

BUYING CITRUS

When buying citrus fruit, look for the heavier ones.

Lighter ones usually indicate thick skin or that it is lacking in juice.

Fish Shashlik

FISH SHASHLIK

Bamboo skewers should be thoroughly soaked in water to prevent burning during cooking.

3 to 4 tablespoons lemon juice

3 to 4 tablespoons sour cream

1 kg large firm-fleshed fish (cut in 5 cm to 6 cm chunks)

bamboo skewers, soaked in water

1 Combine lemon juice and sour cream. Dip each piece of fish in the sauce, then thread onto skewers.

2 Cook shashliks under a griller for 5 to 6 minutes, turning constantly. Baste fish during cooking with any leftover lemon mixture. When ready the fish will be golden. Serve with salad.

SERVES 4 TO 6

POACHED OYSTERS *with* WATERCRESS SAUCE

24 oysters, in the shell

1 to 2 lemons

1 bunch watercress

1 bouquet garni

1 tablespoon finely chopped onion

1 tablespoon finely chopped carrot

½ cup (125 ml) dry white wine

1 cup (250 ml) water

1 Remove oysters from shell and place in a bowl with their liquid.

2 Carefully peel rind of lemons, making sure no pith is included. Cut lemon rind into julienne strips and blanch in boiling water for 3 minutes. Drain, refresh in cold running water and set aside.

3 Pick leaves from watercress. Wash well then blanch in boiling water for 4 minutes. Drain well and purée in a blender or food processor. Measure ⅔ cup (160 ml) of purée and dilute with sufficient cream so that it will lightly coat an oyster. Keep warm.

4 Place remaining ingredients in a pan and simmer for 5 minutes.

5 Remove vegetables and bouquet garni. Add oysters to pan and poach over a gentle heat for 2 minutes. Drain and put oysters back in shells.

6 Divide oysters between 4 serving plates and coat with sauce. Garnish with lemon strips.

SERVES 4

LEMON JUICE

To extract the maximum amount of juice from a lemon, cook in the microwave on HIGH (100%) power for 20 seconds or ensure they are at room temperature and roll on the bench for a few minutes before squeezing.

Poached Oysters with Watercress Sauce

Cut lemon rind into julienne strips

Place remaining ingredients in a pan and simmer for 5 minutes

Drain poached oysters and replace in shells

TO GRATE A COCONUT

Pierce the coconut and pour out liquid. Break the coconut open with a hammer by tapping around the middle. Prise meat out with a knife. Remove skin with a vegetable peeler. Grate in a food processor. This may be frozen.

GRILLED CRAYFISH

2 large green crayfish tails

salt and cayenne pepper

juice 1 lemon

3 to 4 tablespoons olive oil

fresh lemon thyme and rosemary leaves

watercress to garnish

1 Cut crayfish tails in half lengthwise. Season flesh of crayfish with salt and cayenne pepper then brush with lemon juice and olive oil. Sprinkle with a few leaves of the herbs.

2 Place on a grill tray and cook under a preheated griller for 15 to 20 minutes, basting occasionally with a little olive oil.

3 When crayfish are lightly browned, arrange on a serving plate and garnish with watercress. Serve with green salad and crusty bread.

SERVES 4

Lime Rice

LIME RICE

juice of 4 to 5 limes

½ cup (60 g) coconut flesh, grated

1 teaspoon turmeric

½ teaspoon salt

2 cups (250 g) rice, cooked

180 g ghee

½ cup (60 g) mustard seeds

1 cup (125 g) chopped cashews

6 green chillies, seeded and chopped

2 curry leaves, chopped

1 tablespoon finely chopped coriander leaves

GARNISH

1 lime, sliced,

1 Add lime juice, coconut, turmeric and salt to cooked rice. Set aside.

2 Heat ghee. Fry mustard seeds until they pop. Add cashews, chillies and curry leaves. Cook for 3 minutes, stirring. Combine with rice and coriander leaves. Mix well.

3 Cook, covered, over low heat for 15 minutes to heat through. Garnish with lime slices.

SERVES 6

Mix lime juice, coconut, turmeric and salt with cooked rice

Combine cashew nuts with curry leaves and green chillies

Mix chopped coriander leaves with rice and cook slowly for 15 minutes

ROSE GERANIUM SORBET

A cool dessert that is ideal served with spicy meals.

1½ cups (375 g) sugar

2½ cups (625 ml) water

rind and juice 6 lemons

4 rose geranium leaves, lightly crumpled

1 egg white

rose geranium flower and extra leaves, for decoration

1 Place sugar in a medium-sized saucepan with water and lemon rind. Stir over low heat. When sugar has dissolved, bring to the boil.

2 Add crushed leaves. Boil for 6 minutes. Leave to cool.

3 Add lemon juice to cooled syrup. Pour mixture into cold freezer trays or a metal bowl. Place in a freezer until mixture just begins to freeze.

4 Remove and turn into a bowl. Discard geranium leaves. Beat with a whisk until smooth, but not melted.

5 Beat egg white until stiff but not dry. Fold lightly through mixture. Return to tray. Cover. Freeze until firm.

6 Spoon sorbet into chilled glasses. Serve decorated with a rose geranium flower and leaves.

SERVES 2 TO 4

Rose Geranium Sorbet

CANDIED PEEL

Prepare candied peel in your microwave oven by placing thin strips of peel from 2 oranges or lemons (or 1 of each) in a microwave-safe bowl with ½ cup (125 g) caster sugar and ½ cup (125 ml) water. Cook on HIGH (100%) power for 3 minutes, stirring once. Cook for 2 more minutes or until liquid is syrupy. Drain off syrup. Toss peel in some extra caster sugar. When cool, store in an airtight container.

ORANGE SORBET

A light, cool dessert for waistline watchers. If you own an ice cream maker, follow the manufacturer's instructions to freeze this recipe.

10 oranges
1 tablespoon gelatine
2 tablespoons water
½ cup (125 ml) extra water
sugar substitute, to taste
4 egg whites

1 Squeeze juice from oranges and strain.
2 Sprinkle gelatine over 2 tablespoons water. Leave for a few minutes. Place container of gelatine in hot water. Stir until dissolved. Combine with orange juice and extra water. Blend in sweetening to taste.
3 Pour mixture into a cake tin. Freeze until half-frozen. Tip mixture into a bowl.
4 Beat well to break down ice crystals. Place in refrigerator.
5 Whisk egg whites until stiff. Fold into orange juice mixture. Return mixture to freezer. Freeze until half frozen.
6 Turn into a bowl again and beat to break down ice crystals. Refreeze. Beat once more if liked.

SERVES 10 TO 12

SPUN SUGAR

Prepare spun sugar in your microwave oven to give a very attractive garnish to many fruit dishes by dissolving ¼ cup (60 g) caster sugar in ¼ cup (60 ml) boiling water in a microwave-safe bowl. Cook on HIGH (100%) power for 3 to 4 minutes or until syrup is golden. Coat the back of 2 wooden spoons with toffee. Touch and draw spoons apart to form fine toffee strands. If toffee becomes hard, cook on HIGH (100%) power in 20 second bursts until softened.

CHILLED LEMON SOUFFLÉ

375 ml can evaporated skimmed milk
2 tablespoons gelatine
4 tablespoons water
grated rind and juice 4 lemons
powdered or liquid sweetener, to taste
4 kiwi fruit, peeled and sliced

1 Chill evaporated milk in refrigerator overnight.
2 Sprinkle gelatine over water. Leave to stand for a few minutes. Place container of gelatine in hot water. Stir until dissolved.
3 In a large chilled bowl, whisk milk until frothy. Beat in gelatine, lemon rind, juice and sweetener. The dessert should taste lemony – add more juice and rind if necessary.
4 Pour into a serving bowl. Refrigerate until set. To serve, arrange kiwi fruit decoratively on top of soufflé.

SERVES 10 TO 12

LEMON SORBET

4 lemons
2 cups (500 g) sugar
5 cups (1¼ litres) water

1 Peel lemons, remove pith and seeds. Finely chop pulp. Mix with sugar in a saucepan. Allow to stand for 2 hours.
2 Blend in water. Heat slowly, stirring constantly until sugar dissolves.
3 Pour into freezer trays or other suitable containers and freeze for 1 hour.
4 Remove from freezer. Beat vigorously for 2 minutes. Pour back into trays and freeze.

SERVES 6 TO 8

Chilled Lemon Soufflé, Creamy Berries, Orange Sorbet

JUICY FRUIT

To extract the maximum amount of juice from a lemon, cook in the microwave on HIGH (100%) power for 20 seconds or ensure they are at room temperature and roll on the bench for a few minutes before squeezing.

GRAPEFRUIT

Remove flesh easily from a grapefruit by halving and using a grapefruit knife to separate the flesh from the skin. Use a knife to cut between the segments. The flesh will scoop out easily with a spoon.

GLACÉ GRAPEFRUIT

1 orange

2 large grapefruit, halved

½ cup (125 g) caster sugar

3 to 4 tablespoons medium sherry

GARNISH

extra orange and grapefruit segments

shredded peel

mint leaves

4 strawberries

1 Finely grate orange rind. Remove flesh from grapefruit, reserving skin. Segment orange. Dice orange and grapefruit flesh.

2 Blend flesh with sugar, sherry and orange rind. Fill grapefruit halves with mixture. Freeze until set. Garnish with extra orange and grapefruit segments, shredded peel, mint leaves and halved strawberries.

SERVES 4

Glacé Grapefruit

LEMON TART

1 quantity Orange Crust Pastry (see recipe following)

6 eggs

⅔ cup (180 g) sugar

juice 4 lemons

1½ cups (375 ml) cream

100 g butter or margarine, melted

extra cream

1 lemon, sliced, for garnish

1 Roll out pastry on lightly floured board to line a 25 cm flan tin. Cover pastry with baking paper and dried beans or uncooked rice (this is called blind baking). Bake at 200°C (400°F) for 5 minutes. Remove foil and beans. Bake further 5 minutes. Allow to cool.

2 Beat eggs and sugar until light and lemon coloured. Stir in lemon juice, cream and butter. Pour into pastry case.

3 Bake in a moderately slow oven 160°C (325°F) for 45 minutes or until firm. Spread with extra whipped cream. Garnish with slices of lemon.

SERVES 6

ORANGE CRUST PASTRY

1¼ cups (150 g) plain flour, sifted

60 g unsalted butter cubed

60 g margarine

1 teaspoon grated orange rind

2 tablespoons orange juice

1 Place flour in a bowl. Rub in butter and margarine with fingertips until mixture resembles breadcrumbs. Stir in orange rind.

2 Mix orange juice into flour mixture to form a soft dough. Wrap in plastic wrap. Refrigerate for 1 hour.

STEP-BY-STEP TECHNIQUES

LEMON CURD

Orange curd can be made in the same way as lemon curd, using 4 small or 3 large oranges, preferably not too sweet.

4 lemons
180 g butter or margarine
2 cups (500 g) sugar
4 eggs

1 Finely grate rind of 3 lemons. Cut lemons in half. Extract juice and discard pips.

2 Melt butter and sugar in a bowl set over a pan of hot water. Stir until smooth, without boiling. Blend lemon rind and juice into mixture.

3 Beat eggs in another bowl. Whisk them into lemon mixture. Place over low heat. Continue to whisk, without boiling until mixture is thick and creamy.

4 Meanwhile, heat clean jars in a low oven. When curd is ready, pour into jars. Cover curd surface with waxed paper discs.

5 Dampen top side only of cellophane discs and fix them on jars with rubber bands. Leave to cool – the curd will set to a soft jammy texture. Store in a cool place and eat within a month.

MAKES APPROXIMATELY 1 KG

BOTTLING HINTS

When bottling, use clean jars with no cracks or chips.

Seal jars when bottling with sterilised tight-fitting lids (boil them for 5 minutes) or tightly tie waxed or greaseproof paper around neck of jar using elastic bands.

Lemon Curd

Melt butter and sugar in a bowl set over a pan of hot water. Stir until smooth

Blend the finely grated lemon rind and the juice into mixture

Beat the eggs and pour into the lemon mixture, stirring constantly. Continue to stir over a low heat for 30 to 40 minutes until mixture is thick and creamy

Lemon Coconut Slice

2 Press into a Swiss roll tin. Bake at 180°C (350°F) for 20 minutes. While cooking prepare topping.

3 TO PREPARE TOPPING: Combine all ingredients for topping. Spread over base while hot. Allow to set. Cut into fingers.

MAKES APPROXIMATELY 36 FINGERS

CITRUS RING BISCUITS

1 cup (125 g) plain flour

¼ teaspoon allspice

150 g butter or margarine

½ cup (125 g) caster sugar

1 egg

grated rind 1 lemon

1 cup (250 g) ground almonds

2 cups (125 g) fresh breadcrumbs

1 egg yolk, beaten

ICING

2 cups (370 g) icing sugar, sifted

2 tablespoons lemon juice

60 g candied orange and lemon rind

1 Sift flour and spice together. Cream butter and sugar together until light and fluffy. Beat in egg and lemon rind.

2 Fold in flour, ground almonds and breadcrumbs to form dough. Wrap dough in plastic wrap. Chill for 1 hour.

3 Divide dough into 30 pieces and roll each piece until 10 cm long. Brush ends with egg yolk. Join together to form ring. Place on greased baking trays. Bake at 200°C (400°F) for 10 to 15 minutes. Cool on a wire rack.

4 TO PREPARE ICING: Blend together icing sugar and lemon juice. Ice biscuits. Decorate with strips of candied rind.

MAKES 30

LEMON COCONUT SLICE

BASE

125 g butter or margarine, at room temperature

¼ cup (60 g) sugar

½ teaspoon vanilla essence

1 cup (125 g) self-raising flour

½ cup (60 g) grated coconut

TOPPING

60 g butter or margarine, at room temperature

3 tablespoons condensed milk

juice and grated rind 1 lemon

1 cup (180 g) icing sugar

1 cup (90 g) desiccated coconut

1 TO PREPARE BASE: Cream butter and sugar together. Blend in remaining ingredients until well combined.

MIXED FRUIT CUP

1 pawpaw, peeled and seeded

2 bananas, sliced

1 litre water

1 cup (250 g) sugar

1 cup (250 mL) fresh

1/2 cup (125 mL) fresh

pulp 12 passionfruit

2 x 750 mL bottles soda water

ice cubes

10 strawberries, sliced

1 orange, thinly sliced

mint slices

1 Purée pawpaw and bananas in food processor or blender.

2 Boil water and sugar, stirring for 8 to 10 minutes until sugar dissolves and thin syrup is formed. Immediately pour onto orange and lemon juices. Add puréed fruit and passionfruit. Chill until needed.

3 To serve, add soda water and ice cubes and garnish with strawberries, orange slices and mint leaves.

MAKES 3 LITRES

GRAPEFRUIT MARMALADE

Prepare jars by placing in a large pot of boiling water. Simmer for a few minutes. Remove from water with tongs. Place upside down on baking trays. Allow to dry completely in a warm oven.

3 grapefruit, thinly sliced

3 litres water

3 kg sugar

1 teaspoon cream of tartar

1 Cover grapefruit with water. Allow to stand at least 12 hours. Cook, covered, over low heat until tender. Leave until the next day.

2 Bring slowly to the boil. Stir in sugar and cream of tartar. Stir until sugar dissolves.

3 Boil rapidly until marmalade gels when tested on cool saucer. Bottle while hot in warm, sterilised jars. Seal when cold.

MAKES APPROXIMATELY 4 KG

MARMALADE

Marmalade, that favourite breakfast preserve, is made from citrus fruits, using a longer but similar method to jam-making. As with jam, the pectin found in the pith and pips of citrus fruit is the essential setting substance. The setting point is best measured on a sugar thermometer. To test if set, place a little marmalade on a cool plate. If the skin that forms wrinkles when pushed with a finger, the marmalade is set.

Mixed Fruit Cup

Pour syrup into orange and lemon juices

Add puréed fruit

Stir in passionfruit and chill thoroughly

BERRIES

Berries are always associated with the summer months and come in a great variety. The most common, the strawberry, is soft, succulent and seductive. It is available all year round and is used to make many wonderful sweets. Its flavour, as with other berries, varies according to size and ripeness.

Other berries include blackberries, gooseberries, blueberries, mulberries, red and black currants, raspberries and loganberries. Should you desperately want to make something with any of these fruits and they are unavailable, the frozen or canned varieties work well, especially for sauces or purées.

When choosing strawberries, look for evenly coloured, plump fruit with fresh green tops. Avoid punnets containing squashed fruit. They are highly perishable and should be used on the day of purchase, but will keep for a day or two, covered, in the refrigerator. Should any begin to mould, remove immediately as it spreads quickly.

When choosing other berries, look for shiny, plump fruit in punnets without fruit stains.

Raspberries and blueberries can be open frozen and then packed in rigid containers. Blueberries also keep for up to 3 weeks in the refrigerator.

STRAWBERRY

Always wash strawberries before hulling. If the stalks are removed before washing, water may be absorbed into the fruit and ruin the flavour.

BLUEBERRY

Blueberries are used in muffins, pancakes, pies, cakes and biscuits, in sauces and stewed either alone or with apples, pears and quince. They go very well with spices such as cinnamon, coriander, ginger, nutmeg and cardamom. Serve fresh with sour cream or cottage cheese and brown sugar.

BLUEBERRY *and* GOAT'S CHEESE SALAD

1 small loaf French stick

3 tablespoons (50 g) butter

16 slices goat's cheese, 1 cm thick

1 coral lettuce, washed

1 cos lettuce, washed

2 valencia oranges, segmented

1 grapefruit, segmented

150 g snow peas, blanched

½ cup (60 g) blueberries

2 tablespoons walnut oil

2 teaspoons white vinegar

1 teaspoon French mustard

1 Slice French stick into 16 x 1 cm slices. Spread each slice with a little butter. Place a slice of cheese on each. Place on a baking tray. Bake at 200°C (400°F) for 15 minutes. Allow to cool.

2 Tear lettuce into bite-sized pieces. Arrange lettuce, citrus segments, snow peas and blueberries on serving plates. Garnish with toasted goat's cheese.

3 Combine walnut oil, vinegar and mustard. Sprinkle over salad.

SERVES 8

SUMMER SALAD *with* RASPBERRY VINAIGRETTE

1 mignonette lettuce, washed and dried

1 butter lettuce, washed and dried

1 small Spanish onion, thinly sliced

1 barbeque chicken, skin removed and cut into bite-sized pieces

1 mango, peeled and sliced

1 pawpaw, peeled and sliced

½ cup (60 g) blueberries

½ cup (60 g) halved pecans, toasted

RASPBERRY VINAIGRETTE

½ cup (125 ml) olive oil

¼ cup (60 g) raspberries

1 tablespoon white wine vinegar

2 teaspoons honey

1 teaspoon sesame oil

¼ teaspoon Tabasco sauce

salt and freshly ground black pepper to taste

1 Arrange all ingredients for salad in a serving bowl. Toss well. Cover. Refrigerate until required.

2 TO PREPARE RASPBERRY VINAIGRETTE: Place all ingredients in a food processor or blender. Process until smooth. Pour over salad just before serving. Toss well.

SERVES 4 TO 6

BLACKBERRY

Blackberries are very nourishing, containing a high proportion of calcium and vitamin B1. They can be served fresh or in jams or tarts, etc. Because of their 'pippy' texture, a lot of blackberry cooking requires straining the pulp and using the extracted juice.

RASPBERRY

Raspberries are one of the sweetest and most delectable of berries. Raspberries can be eaten fresh, or served in compotes, cakes, flans, tarts, pancakes, jams or jellies. Raspberries puréed with cream are a tasty dressing for fruit desserts.

STEP-BY-STEP TECHNIQUES

ICED SUMMER SALAD

125 g strawberries, hulled

1 peach, peeled and seeded

1 banana, peeled

2 teaspoons sugar

250 g cream cheese

2 tablespoons lemon juice

½ teaspoon ground ginger

2 tablespoons cream, whipped

¼ cup (30 g) chopped hazelnuts

shredded lettuce

prepared vinaigrette dressing

1 Dice fruit. Sprinkle with sugar.

2 Beat cream cheese with lemon juice and ginger.

3 Fold in cream, fruit and nuts.

4 Pour mixture into 4 individual moulds. Freeze for 1 to 2 hours or until firm.

5 Dip each mould into warm water. Turn salad into a bed of shredded lettuce. Serve immediately with vinaigrette dressing.

SERVES 4

Iced Summer Salad

Sprinkle diced fruit with sugar

Fold in cream, nuts and fruit

Spoon mixture into individual moulds

until dough is very smooth. Add extra flour if necessary.

4 Roll out until thin. Cut into small rounds (about 5 to 6 cm in diameter).

5 To Prepare Filling: Place fruit in a pan with sugar. Bring to the boil, stirring constantly. Take care that it does not burn.

6 To Complete: Place about 1 teaspoon of prepared filling on each round. Fold over. Pinch edges to seal. Pull out ends to form horns and curl under the base of dumpling.

7 Place on floured board with tails underneath until ready to cook.

8 Half fill a large saucepan with water. Bring to the boil. Drop in about 10 dumplings at a time. Simmer for 5 to 10 minutes, or until they rise to the surface.

9 Use a large perforated spoon to remove when cooked. Drain. Serve with extra fruit filling and cream.

Fruit-filled Dumplings

FRUIT-FILLED DUMPLINGS

PASTRY

3 cups (375 g) plain flour, sifted

4 eggs yolks

2 cups (500 ml) warm milk

FILLING

600 g pitted cherries, strawberries, blueberries or pitted plums, washed

1 cup (250 g) sugar, or as required

1 To Prepare Pastry: Place flour in a large mixing bowl. Make a well in the centre. Whisk egg yolks and milk. Pour into well.

2 Slowly, with a wooden spoon fold in flour until the dough forms a ball. Knead well. Cover with a cloth. Set aside for about 30 minutes.

3 Transfer dough to a floured board. Knead

❦ **COEUR À LA CRÈME**

Coeur à la Crème moulds are white, heart-shaped moulds available from cookware and department stores in the gourmet cookware section. Small ramekin moulds may be used as a substitute.

COEUR *à la* CRÈME

375 g cream-style cottage cheese

250 g cream cheese

¼ cup (60 ml) thickened cream, whipped

1 tablespoon icing sugar, sifted

icing sugar, extra

1 punnet raspberries or 250 g frozen, thawed

1 punnet fresh strawberries, for garnish

1 Cream together the 2 cheeses. Fold in cream and icing sugar.

2 Line 6 Coeur à la Crème moulds with muslin. Stand on a small tray. Spoon cheese mixture into moulds. Smooth top. Refrigerate overnight.

3 Unmould onto 6 dessert plates. Remove muslin. Sift extra icing sugar over the top.

4 Purée raspberries in a food processor. Sweeten to taste with icing sugar if desired. Spoon sauce around each Coeur à la Creme. Garnish with strawberries.

SERVES 6

Coeur à la Crème

HULLING
STRAWBERRIES

Remove strawberry stalks
(hulling) by twisting the
leaves.

BERRY MUFFINS

3 cups (375 g) plain flour

1 tablespoon baking powder

½ cup (125 g) sugar

½ cup (90g) brown sugar

½ cup (125 g) butter or margarine, melted

3 eggs

1 cup (250 ml) milk

1 to 1½ cups (250 g) berries in season

icing sugar

1 Sift flour and baking powder into a bowl. Stir in sugars.

2 Combine butter, eggs and milk. Stir into dry ingredients until just blended.

3 Fold in berries very lightly. If large berries such as strawberries are used, cut into dice.

4 Spoon into greased muffin tins until two-thirds full. Bake at 200°C (400°F) for 15 to 20 minutes or until golden. Sprinkle with icing sugar while hot. Serve hot with butter.

NOTE: Do not worry if all the flour is not mixed in – 16 strokes is usually enough. This helps to give the characteristic texture of muffins.

MAKES 20 TO 24

CREAMY BERRIES

BERRY PURÉES

Berry purées make
delicious dressings. Add
a little to your favourite
vinaigrette for a
refreshing change.

3 punnets ripe strawberries

sugar, to taste

2 tablespoons gelatine

4 tablespoons water

6 egg whites

1 Purée berries with sugar. Sprinkle gelatine over water and leave to stand for 5 minutes. Place container of gelatine in hot water to dissolve then stir gelatine into purée.

2 Whisk egg whites to form stiff peaks; fold into berries. Taste and adjust for sweetness. Spoon into serving bowl, cover and chill.

SERVES 10 TO 12

MIXED BERRY PUDDING

8 slices white bread, crusts removed

2 tablespoons brandy

750 g mixed berries, eg. strawberries, raspberries, blueberries, mulberries (see note)

½ cup (125 g) sugar (see note)

2 tablespoons water

cream to serve

1 Cut bread into fingers. Cover base and sides of a 4-cup soufflé dish with bread, saving enough pieces to form a lid.

2 Drizzle brandy over the bread on the base. Set aside.

3 Place fruit in a large pan with sugar and water. Cook over a very low heat until the sugar has dissolved and the fruit is soft but not mushy (there should be plenty of juice).

4 Strain the fruit. Reserve juice. Drizzle 1 tablespoon of juice over base of pudding. Spoon the fruit into the bread case.

5 Pour over all but ¼ cup (60 ml) juice. Fold bread over fruit. Top with remaining bread fingers. Pour over remaining juice.

6 Place a plate, small enough to fit inside the rim of the dish, on top of the pudding. Press down with heavy cans or weights. Refrigerate overnight.

7 Just before serving, remove the weights and plate. Invert onto serving dish. Serve with cream.

NOTE: If canned fruit is used, use juice and reduce sugar to ¼ cup.

SERVES 4 TO 6

MAKING FOOD PROCESSOR PASTRY

When using a food processor to make pastry, be careful not
to overmix as the pastry will be tough. It is best to use the
"pulse" to help prevent this.

BERRY FLAN

PASTRY

1½ cups (180 g) plain flour

2 tablespoons caster sugar

125 g butter or margarine, cubed

1 egg yolk

1 tablespoon ice water

FILLING

250 g cream cheese, softened

½ cup (125 ml) sour cream

½ cup (90 g) icing sugar

1 tablespoon brandy

TOPPING

1 punnet raspberries

1 punnet blueberries

extra icing sugar

1 TO PREPARE PASTRY: Place flour and sugar into a food processor. Process until combined. Gradually add butter to the flour. Process until it resembles breadcrumbs.

2 Add egg yolk. Process until combined. With the motor running, add only enough water until pastry forms a soft ball.

3 Turn mixture out onto a lightly floured board. Knead lightly. Wrap in plastic wrap. Rest for 30 minutes. Roll out pastry to fit a 28 cm flan.

4 Bake blind at 200°C (400°F) for 10 minutes. Remove paper and rice, bake a further 5 minutes or until golden. Remove from oven. Cool.

5 TO PREPARE FILLING: Place softened cream cheese and sour cream into food processor. Process until smooth. Add icing sugar and brandy. Combine well. Transfer to a bowl. Chill.

6 TO PREPARE TOPPING: Spoon filling into pastry case. Arrange berries over the filling. Lightly dust with extra icing sugar. Chill.

SERVES 12

TO BAKE BLIND

Cover pastry with baking paper and dried beans or uncooked rice. Bake at 200°C (400°F) for 5 minutes. Remove paper and beans. Bake further 5 minutes. Allow to cool.

Berry Flan

STONE FRUIT

With the summer comes the mouthwatering aroma and delectable flavour of stone fruits, which include all-time favourites like cherries, peaches, nectarines, apricots, plums and loquats. These fruits are perfect additions to all types of summer cooking, whether raw or cooked.

When purchasing cherries, look for shiny, plump, unblemished fruit, avoiding any that are split or soft. They will keep for several days in the refrigerator.

Peaches come in many varieties, but they all have either yellow or white flesh. If the flesh adheres to the stone they are known as cling stone, and if it comes away cleanly they are known as freestone. They are delicious grilled, poached or used to decorate tarts. Look for firm fruit with yellow or white beneath the rose blush. They will keep refrigerated for about a week.

Plums also come in many varieties and are great puréed, poached, in jams, sorbets, ice creams or as a sauce to accompany pork, duck or goose.

Choose undamaged fruit that is not too soft. The same applies to nectarines and apricots.

Cherry Soup

CHERRY SOUP

500 g ripe cherries, stoned
3 cups (750 ml) water
½ cup (125 g) sugar
⅓ cup (80 ml) lemon juice
fresh mint or parsley for garnish
plain yoghurt (optional)

TO STONE CHERRIES

To stone cherries, push stone through with a skewer or use a cherry stoner.

1 Bring cherries, water, sugar and lemon juice to boil. Simmer gently for 10 minutes. Allow to cool.
2 Purée in a food processor. Chill thoroughly.
3 Serve garnished with mint or parsley and, if liked, a teaspoon of yoghurt in each bowl.
NOTE: This recipe may also be served over crushed ice.

SERVES 6

PORK ROAST *with* CHERRY SAUCE

3 to 4 kg pork loin
2 cups (500 ml) boiling water
2 tablespoons oil
1 tablespoon coarse salt
6 cloves garlic
12 small bay leaves

CHERRY SAUCE
½ cup (60 g) pitted cherries
¼ cup (60 ml) corn syrup
2 tablespoons vinegar
salt and freshly ground pepper, to taste
pinch nutmeg
pinch cinnamon
pinch ground cloves

1 Deeply score rind of pork into 1.5 cm strips. Place pork loin, skin side down, in a pan. Pour in boiling water. Bake at 200°C (400°F) for 15 minutes. Remove pan. Drain off liquid, reserving it for basting.
2 Add oil to pan. Rub pork skin with salt. Insert cloves and bay leaves in score marks. Roast pork, skin side up at 190°C (375°F) for 3 to 3 ½ hours. Baste with drained liquid every 30 minutes.
3 When cooked, remove from pan. Cover. Allow to stand for 20 minutes before carving.
4 TO PREPARE CHERRY SAUCE: Combine sauce ingredients in a saucepan. Bring to boil. Simmer for 3 minutes or until heated through.
5 Carve pork. Serve sliced with Cherry Sauce.

SERVES 12

BREAST of DUCKLING with APRICOT SAUCE

The stock and sauce can be prepared in advance. The duck can be served warm or cool.

1 x 3 kg duckling

1 bay leaf

few celery leaves

10 black peppercorns

few sprigs parsley

1 small onion, peeled and sliced

3 tablespoons white wine

mustard cress or watercress to garnish

APRICOT SAUCE

¾ cup (90 g) dried apricots

salt and freshly ground pepper to taste

juice of ½ lemon

1 tablespoon brandy

1 Dislocate the wing and leg joints of the duck. Cut off. Cut off the wing tips. Reserve. Keep the wings and legs for another recipe.

2 Cut the breast away from the backbone, leaving whole. Place the wing tips and backbone in a pan. Cover with water and bring to the boil. Lift off any foam. Add bay leaf, celery leaves, peppercorns, parsley, onion and wine. Simmer, partially covered, for 1 to 1½ hours.

3 TO PREPARE APRICOT SAUCE: Strain reserving 2 cups of stock. Soak the apricots in stock for 1 to 2 hours.

4 Cook the apricots until tender. Purée in a food processor. Add seasonings and lemon juice.

5 Stir in brandy. If the sauce is a little thick, thin it down with extra stock.

6 Prick the duck breast with a skewer. Season lightly with salt. Place in a pan. Roast at 190°C (375°F) for 10 minutes. Reduce the heat to 180°C (350°F). Bake for

another 20 minutes or until cooked when tested.

7 Remove the breast. Let it cool to room temperature. Carefully peel off all the skin. Slice flesh neatly.

8 Pour ⅓ cup of sauce into 4 plates. Arrange overlapping sliced of duck and skin on top. Garnish with mustard cress or watercress. Serve any remaining sauce separately.

SERVES 4

CHICKEN with PLUM and LYCHEE SAUCE

1 x 1.5 kg chicken, cut in bite-sized pieces

½ cup Chinese plum sauce

1 clove garlic, crushed

1 tablespoon soy sauce

1 teaspoon minced ginger

¼ teaspoon chilli sauce

1 tablespoon oil

225 g can lychees, drained, reserving ¼ cup (60 ml) juice

¼ cup (60 ml) water chestnuts

¼ cup (30 g) bamboo shoots, sliced

2 tablespoons cornflour

1 teaspoon sesame oil

1 Remove skin from chicken pieces. Marinate for 2 hours with plum sauce, garlic, soy, ginger and chilli sauce. Drain. Reserve liquid.

2 Add oil to wok. Heat. Stir-fry chicken pieces. Cover with lid. Simmer 5 minutes.

3 Add marinade juices. Cover. Cook a further 5 minutes. Add lychees, water chestnuts and bamboo shoots. Stir-fry 1 to 2 minutes.

4 Combine reserved lychee juice and cornflour. Stir into wok. Bring to the boil. Simmer 3 minutes. Stir through sesame oil. Serve hot with steamed rice.

SERVES 6

TO MAKE A COULIS

Make delicious coulis by placing 250 g of fruit of choice in a food processor or blender with 1 tablespoon of orange juice or liqueur of choice (eg. Grand Marnier, brandy, etc.). Process until smooth. Serve with sweet or savoury dishes or just simply over ice cream.

WHEN FRESH IS UNAVAILABLE

Frozen or canned varieties of fruit may be substituted for fresh if fresh is unavailable

TO STONE FRUIT

Stone fruit by running a
knife around the centre.
Twist apart. Remove
stone.

STORING FRUIT

If storing fruit in the
refrigerator, remove about
30 minutes before serving
to ensure its full flavour
is appreciated.

PLUM FLAN

PASTRY

1⅓ cups (180 g) wholemeal flour

90 g butter, cubed

1 egg yolk

a little milk

FILLING

3 egg yolks

300 ml natural yoghurt

¼ cup (90 g) honey

½ teaspoon powdered cinnamon

500 g small plums, halved and stoned

½ cup (90 g) blanched almonds

1 tablespoon brown sugar

1 TO PREPARE PASTRY: Sift flour into a
bowl. Rub in butter. Add egg yolk and
enough milk to form firm dough.

2 Roll out to line a 20 cm flan dish. Prick
base a few times with a fork.

3 TO PREPARE FILLING: Beat yolks with
yoghurt, honey and cinnamon. Pour into
pastry case.

4 Arrange plums, cut side down, in yoghurt
mixture. Bake at 200°C (400°F) for 35 to 40
minutes or until custard is set.

5 Sprinkle with nuts and brown sugar.
Brown under a hot grill.

SERVES 6

SUMMER FRUIT
with SOUR CREAM

6 peaches, plums, apricots, nectarines or
combination, peeled, halved and stoned

2 teaspoons caster sugar

¼ cup (60 ml) Grand Marnier

300 ml sour cream

½ cup (90 g) brown sugar

¼ cup (30 g) flaked almonds, toasted

1 Place fruit cut side up in an ovenproof
dish. Sprinkle with sugar.

2 Pour over Grand Marnier. Cover with
plastic wrap. Refrigerate for several hours or
overnight.

3 Remove from refrigerator 2 to 3 hours
before serving. Just before serving, cover
with sour cream. Sprinkle with brown sugar.

4 Place under a hot grill until sugar
caramelises. Top with almonds. Serve
immediately.

SERVES 6

RUBY CLAFOUTIS

750 g plums

½ cup (60 g) plain flour

½ cup (125 g) sugar

4 eggs

1 cup (250 ml) milk

2 tablespoons brandy

2 tablespoons flaked almonds

extra sugar

1 Place plums into a large saucepan of
boiling water. Simmer 2 to 3 minutes until
just tender. Strain. Plunge into cold water to
cool.

2 Halve plums. Remove stems and stones.
Transfer to a lightly buttered ovenproof dish.
Place flour and sugar into a bowl. Beat in
eggs, one at a time. Add half the milk. Beat
for 5 minutes. Stir in the remaining milk
and brandy.

3 Pour mixture over the plums. Sprinkle
with flaked almonds. Bake at 180°C (350°F)
for 40 to 45 minutes. Sprinkle with extra
sugar. Serve hot with cream.

NOTE: Apricots may be substituted for
plums if desired.

SERVES 4

FRESH FRUIT SHORTCAKE

125 g butter or margarine

¼ cup sugar

4 egg yolks

1½ cups plain flour, sifted

TOPPING

2½ cups cream, whipped

2 cups chopped fruit (peaches, nectarines, plums, apricots)

2 nectarines, halved, seeded and finely sliced

1 Cream butter and sugar together until light and fluffy. Add egg yolks one at a time. Beat well after each addition. Mix in flour until well combined.

2 Knead dough on a lightly floured working surface. Place on greased pizza tray, using your knuckles or fingertips to press out to fit tray.

3 Bake blind (see Pear Tart with Frangipani Cream) at 180°C (350°F) for 20 to 25 minutes or until lightly browned. Remove from oven. When cold, gently lift shortcake onto serving dish.

4 TO PREPARE TOPPING: Combine cream and fruit. Spoon onto shortcake base. Arrange nectarine slices on cream with skin-side showing. Serve slightly chilled.

SERVES 10 TO 12

The shortcake base may be cooked up to 2 days ahead of time and stored in a covered container.

Peach Chocolate Cups

5 Spoon into individual chocolate cases. Chill for at least 2 hours before serving. Garnish with mint leaves.

SERVES 4

PEACH *and* PLUM FROZEN TERRINE

500 g peaches, peeled and stoned

½ cup (125 ml) orange juice

¼ cup (60 g) caster sugar

rind and juice of 1 lemon

500 g plums, peeled and stoned

½ cup (125 ml) orange juice, extra

¼ cup (60 g) caster sugar, extra

2 tablespoons port

1 Place peaches, orange juice, sugar and lemon rind and juice in a food processor or blender. Process until smooth. Pour into a Swiss roll tin. Freeze.

2 Repeat with remaining ingredients. Freeze.

3 When both purées are icy but not solid, spoon half of the peach mixture into the base of a plastic wrap-lined loaf tin. Smooth top.

4 Top with half the plum mixture. Smooth top. Repeat with remaining mixture to make 4 layers. Cover the surface with plastic wrap. Freeze overnight.

5 Remove the plastic from the top. Invert the terrine onto a serving plate. Remove remaining plastic.

6 Cut into 1 cm slices with a warm knife to serve. Garnish with slices of peaches and plums and a sprig of mint.

SERVES 8

PEACH CHOCOLATE CUPS

300 g dark chocolate, melted

6 peaches, peeled, seeded and roughly chopped

juice 1 large lime

⅔ cup (160 ml) natural yoghurt

1 teaspoon gelatine

2 teaspoons cold water

4 mint sprigs, to garnish

MELTING CHOCOLATE

Melt chocolate in your microwave in a microwave-safe bowl in short bursts on MEDIUM power (50%). Stir between each burst.

1 Light brush 4 x 10 cm individual tart tins with oil. Spoon 2 tablespoons melted chocolate into bottom of each. Using a pastry brush, spread chocolate evenly around the base and sides of tin.

2 Allow to set in refrigerator. Brush with extra chocolate if the cases are too thin. When solid, lift from tins carefully so as not to break edges.

3 Purée peaches, lime juice and yoghurt in a food processor. Soften gelatine in cold water. Stir over a bowl of hot water until dissolved. Whisk into peach mixture.

Fruity Brandy Snap Baskets

Brandy Snap Baskets may be made several days in advance and stored in an airtight container.

Brandy Snap Baskets

60 g butter or margarine

¼ cup (45 g) brown sugar

¼ cup (90 g) golden syrup

¼ cup (30 g) plain flour

½ teaspoon ground ginger

1 teaspoon lemon juice

¼ teaspoon vanilla essence

Filling

1 tablespoon rum (see note)

200 g mascarpone (see note)

sliced stoned fruit of choice

1 To Prepare Brandy Snap Baskets: Place butter, sugar and syrup in a small saucepan. Heat gently until butter has melted and sugar has dissolved. Cool.

2 Sift flour and ginger together. Stir into butter mixture with lemon juice and vanilla.

3 Place teaspoonfuls of the mixture onto greased trays. Allow room for spreading.

4 Bake at 180°C (350°F) for about 5 minutes or until golden. Allow to cool on trays for 1 minute.

5 Remove from trays with spatula. Place over a greased up-turned glass. Shape into a basket with fingers. Cool completely. Continue with remaining mixture.

6 To Prepare Filling: Blend rum into mascarpone. Spoon into baskets. Top with fruit just before serving.

Note: Other liqueurs may be used to flavour mascarpone. Mascarpone is an Italian-style cream cheese available from delicatessens.

Makes about 12

Blackforest Crepe Cake

Crepe Mixture

2 cups (250 g) plain flour

2½ cups (625 ml) milk

2 eggs

30 g butter or margarine

Filling

440 g can pitted black cherries

¼ cup (60 ml) orange-flavoured liqueur

2 tablespoons sugar

2 tablespoons cornflour

1 cup (250 ml) cream, whipped

3 tablespoons almond flakes, toasted

1 To Prepare Crepes: Sift flour into a bowl. Blend in milk and eggs to form a smooth batter.

2 Grease crepe pan with butter. Pour ¼ cup (60 ml) crepe mixture into hot pan. Turn pan to cover base thinly with mixture. Pour off excess. Cook for 1 to 2 minutes. Turn to cook other side.

3 Continue until 15 to 20 crepes have been made. Layer crepes between paper towels. Allow to cool.

4 To Prepare Filling: Place cherries with juice, liqueur, sugar and cornflour in saucepan. Bring to boil, stirring. Allow to thicken. Cool.

5 Spreading filling between each layer, form crepes into dome shape.

6 Coat outside of crepes with cream. Pipe crown of rosettes on top of cake. Decorate sides of cake with toasted almonds. Refrigerate until serving. Serve sliced.

7 To toast almonds, place in a dry frying pan. Toss over a low heat until golden. Remove from pan. Cool.

Serves 10 to 12

Peel peaches by dipping in boiling water for 30 seconds to 1 minute. Place immediately in cold water. The skin will come away easily. Apricots and plums are peeled in the same way.

Crepe Batter

Crepe batter should be the consistency of pouring cream. To achieve this, add more liquid as required.

TO PREPARE SUGAR SYRUP

Heat ½ cup sugar with ¼ cup water, stirring until sugar has dissolved. Bring to the boil. Simmer for 2 to 3 minutes.

PEACH MOUSSE

2 ripe peaches

1 tablespoon lemon juice

almond or orange liqueur (optional)

1 cup (125 ml) cream, chilled

2 egg whites

¼ cup (60 g) sugar

Amaretti biscuits, for garnish

1 Blanch peaches in boiling water for 30 seconds. Remove, plunge into cold water then carefully peel. Slice peaches. Purée in food processor with lemon juice and liqueur.

2 Beat the cream until stiff. Chill. Beat egg whites until stiff peaks form, gradually adding the sugar until glossy.

3 Fold the whipped cream and meringue mixtures into the peach purée.

4 Spoon mousse into custard cups or glasses. Freeze 1 hour then transfer to refrigerator for 2 hours. Serve chilled but not hard, garnish with Amaretti.

SERVES 6

POACHED PEACHES

4 peaches

¼ cup (30 g) desiccated coconut

¼ cup (30 g) ground almonds

1 egg yolk

½ teaspoon finely grated orange rind

30 g butter or margarine

1 cup (250 ml) white wine

1 cinnamon stick

1 Plunge peaches into boiling water for 30 seconds. Drain. Cover with cold water. Peel, cut in half and remove stones.

2 Place peaches, cut side up, in an ovenproof dish. Combine coconut, almonds, egg yolk and orange rind. Spoon into peach cavities. Dot with butter.

3 Pour in wine and add cinnamon stick. Bake, covered, at 180°C (350°F) for 20 minutes or until peaches are tender. Remove cinnamon stick. Serve warm.

SERVES 4 TO 8

PEACH *and* DATE SLICES

1½ cups (180 g) self-raising wholemeal flour

1 cup (150 g) brown sugar

425 g can peach slices, drained and roughly chopped

½ cup (90 g) dates, finely chopped

½ cup (60 g) desiccated coconut

½ cup (60 g) hazelnuts, finely chopped

180 g butter or margarine, melted

1 Sift flour into bowl. Add sugar, peaches, dates, coconut and hazelnuts. Mix in butter. Pour into a greased lamington tin.

2 Bake at 190°C (375°F) for 25 minutes. Allow to cool in tin, then cut in pieces. Store in an airtight container.

MAKES ABOUT 24

HONEYED FRUITS

2 kg stone fruits (plums, cherries, apricots and peaches)

2 tablespoons honey

600 ml rosé wine

1 Prepare fruit. Slice or halve according to size. Layer fruit in large glass serving dish.

2 Stir honey into wine. Pour over fruit. Leave overnight in refrigerator. Serve with yoghurt or cream.

SERVES 12

PEACH ICE CREAM *with* FRESH PEACHES

3 large peaches
1½ (375 ml) cups cream
1 tablespoon Grand Marnier
½ cup (125 ml) sugar
¼ cup (60 ml) sugar syrup (see note)
1 tablespoon chopped pistachio nuts

1 Pour boiling water over 1 peach in a bowl. Stand 1 minute. Drain. Plunge into cold water then remove skin and stone. Mash to make ½ cup.

2 Combine peach pulp with cream, 2 teaspoons Grand Marnier and sugar in food processor. Blend until smooth and the sugar is dissolved. Pour into the container of an ice cream hand churn or into a freezer tray.

3 Churn or freeze until of ice cream consistency. If a freezer tray is used, beat lightly halfway through freezing. Place freezer wrap over trays to prevent ice crystals forming.

4 If a churn is used, remove from churn and store in a covered container in the freezer until required. Scoop into ice cream balls and place on a metal slide covered with plastic wrap.

5 Just before serving, peel the remaining peaches (as described previously) and cut each into 8 slices. Place in a bowl. Marinate with sugary syrup and the remaining Grand Marnier. Cover to prevent fruit discolouring.

6 Place 2 scoops ice cream in individual bowls. Arrange the fruit slices on top. Sprinkle with pistachio nuts. Serve with sponge finger biscuits if liked.

SERVES 4 TO 6

Peach Ice Cream
with Fresh Peaches

Step-by-Step Techniques

Plum Jam

2 kg blood plums

2½ cups (625 ml) water

2 kg sugar

1 Chop plums into sections and remove and preserve stones. Place fruit and water in a large saucepan. Simmer gently until plums are tender.

2 Meanwhile crack a few of the stones. Remove kernels. Blanch them with boiling water and remove skins. Add kernels to fruit.

3 Remove pan from heat. Add sugar. Stir until completely dissolved. Return pan to heat. Boil rapidly, stirring continuously and removing any scum that rises, until jam reaches setting point (see Lemon Marmalade) or temperature on sugar thermometer reaches 105°C.

4 Remove from heat. Allow jam to cool for about 10 minutes before filling jars. Allow jam to cool thoroughly before sealing.

MAKES ABOUT 3 KG

Chop plums into sections and remove stones

Simmer plums until tender

Remove pan from heat, add sugar and stir until dissolved. Return to heat and boil.

CHERRIES *in* BRANDY

1½ cups (375 g) sugar

1 cup (250 ml) water

strip of orange or lemon peel

1.5 kg cherries, stoned

brandy

5 cloves

2.5 cm piece cinnamon

1 Place sugar, water and peel into a saucepan. Bring to the boil, stirring until sugar dissolves. Reduce heat. Simmer for 10 minutes, without stirring.

2 Add cherries. Simmer for a further 5 minutes, reserving syrup. Spoon cherries into clean dry jars. Half fill jars with brandy. Add cloves and cinnamon. Top up jars with reserved syrup.

3 Seal jars. Label. Store in a cool place for 1 month before using. Preserves will keep for up to 12 months.

NOTE: Other stone fruits may be used. Peel, halve and stone before continuing.

MAKES 1.5 KG

PLUM BUTTER

1 kg plums

sugar

1 teaspoon ground cinnamon

1 Barely cover plums with water. Cook, covered, very slowly until tender. Push through sieve, discarding stones.

2 Measure purée. For every 2½ cups mix in 500 g sugar. Slowly heat, stirring until sugar dissolves.

3 Add cinnamon. Boil for about ¾ hour until a spoon drawn across pan leaves a clean line behind it. Pour into warm sterilised jars. Seal.

MAKES ABOUT 3 CUPS

APRICOT CHUTNEY

1 kg apricots, halved and stoned

2 cups (300 g) brown sugar

2 onions, thinly sliced

¾ cup (125 g) sultanas

1 tablespoon salt

1 teaspoon coriander seeds

½ teaspoon ground ginger

250 ml white wine vinegar

1 Simmer all ingredients together until apricots are soft – about 15 to 20 minutes. Transfer apricots to warm, sterilised jars.

2 Boil rest of chutney until it is thick and syrupy. Pour over apricots. Seal.

NOTE: Peaches may be substituted for apricots.

MAKES ABOUT 4 CUPS

PEACH CHUTNEY

5 kg peaches, peeled, halved and stoned

1.25 kg sugar

250 g salt

30 g allspice

30 g cloves

30 g garlic, peeled and chopped

15 g peppercorns, ground

2 x 750 ml bottles white vinegar

1 Boil all ingredients together for 3 hours or until thick. Pour into warm, sterilised jars. Seal.

NOTE: Plums may be substituted for peaches.

MAKES ABOUT 10 CUPS

FRUITS
from the
VINE

Grapes, passionfruit and kiwi fruit fall into this category. Melons are also grown on vines, but we have devoted a whole chapter to them alone.

Grapes have been cultivated for thousands of years, mainly to produce wine. Today, the grapes we consume with relish are specifically grown for eating. Perfect with cheese, in desserts or used to enhance certain seafood or chicken dishes and salads, grapes also make lovely garnishes. Handle these delicate fruits with care and look for bunches without any trace of browning.

The kiwi fruit has a fuzzy brown skin which hides its brilliant green, juicy flesh. Perfect as a garnish, kiwi purée is also delicious in mousse, ice cream, sorbet and jam.

The passionfruit vine that adorns many a garden fence bears a fragrant fruit with a distinctive sweet-sour flavour. This is one fruit where crunchy seeds are designed to be eaten! Look for purple fruit with a wrinkled skin. Use them as a garnish or to make jams, drinks or ices.

PERFECT CHOICE

Purchase kiwi fruit when firm and allow to ripen at room temperature. Kiwi fruit are ripe when the flesh gives a little between the fingers.

NOTE

Any blue cheese may be substituted for Roquefort.

Turkey and Roquefort Salad with Cranberry Dressing

TURKEY *and* ROQUEFORT SALAD *with* CRANBERRY DRESSING

3 cups (300 g) diced cooked turkey

1 cup (30 g) shredded lettuce

1 cup (60 g) diced celery

½ cup (60 g) seedless grapes

½ cup (60 g) toasted pecans, chopped

45 g Roquefort cheese, crumbled (see note)

CRANBERRY DRESSING

250 g jar cranberry sauce

¼ cup (90 ml) dark soy sauce

1 small clove garlic, crushed

2 tablespoons lemon juice

2 tablespoons sherry

1 tablespoon vegetable oil

1 Combine turkey, lettuce, celery, grapes and pecans. Pile mixture into shallow serving dish. Crumble Roquefort cheese over top of salad.

2 TO PREPARE CRANBERRY DRESSING: Combine all ingredients in a small saucepan. Heat until well blended. Serve separately in a sauce boat.

SERVES 6

KIWI *and* CASHEW SALAD

few lettuce leaves

4 kiwi fruit, peeled and sliced

2 oranges, segmented

6 radishes, thinly sliced

100 g mushrooms, sliced

1 small cucumber, sliced

2 sticks celery, sliced

¼ cup (30 g) cashews

vinaigrette dressing to taste

1 Tear lettuce into pieces. Toss all salad ingredients in a salad bowl with nuts and vinaigrette dressing.

SERVES 4

CHICKEN LIVERS VERONIQUE

750 g chicken livers

2 tablespoons chopped shallots

seasoned flour (see note)

60 g butter or margarine

3 tablespoons white wine

3 tablespoons chicken stock

1 tablespoon fruit juice

1½ cups (180 g) seedless grapes

4 to 6 tablespoons sour cream

finely chopped parsley to garnish

1 Rinse chicken livers, pat dry. Dust with seasoned flour. Shake off excess.

2 Sauté shallots and livers in butter over a medium heat for 6 to 8 minutes. Pour in white wine, stock and fruit juice. Bring to the boil.

3 Add grapes. Reduce heat. Cook, covered, for 3 minutes.

4 Stir in sour cream. Reheat gently. Serve sprinkled with finely chopped parsley.

SERVES 6

BEEF CASSEROLE *with* KIWI FRUIT

1 kg round or topside steak

2 to 3 kiwi fruit, peeled and sliced

1 tablespoon oil

1 onion, sliced

1 red capsicum, sliced

1 tablespoon flour

1 cup (250 ml) beef stock

1 tablespoon soy sauce

1 tablespoon French mustard

freshly ground black pepper to taste

1 Rub meat all over with a few slices of kiwi fruit. Cut meat into 6 pieces. Allow to stand for 10 to 15 minutes.

2 Brown steaks in hot oil. Remove meat. Saute onions and capsicum until tender.

3 Stir in flour. Cook, stirring, until brown. Stir in stock, soy sauce, mustard and pepper.

4 Return meat to pan with remaining kiwi fruit. Simmer, covered, over low heat for 1 hour or until tender.

SERVES 6

Chicken Livers Veronique

KIWI FRUIT COOK'S TIP

The flesh of kiwi fruit contains an enzyme that tenderises meat.

HOW TO MAKE SEASONED FLOUR

Seasoned flour is plain flour combined with seasonings of choice, eg. salt, pepper, ground ginger, dried herbs, to give added flavour.

GRILLED SPATCHCOCKS *with* GRAPES

To Skin and Seed Grapes

To Skin and Seed Grapes

Grapes are best skinned and seeded when used in cooking recipes. To skin grapes, dip in boiling water for a few seconds. Skin is easily peeled back with the fingers. Remove seeds by making a slit in one side and flicking out the seeds with the point of a knife.

Grilled Spatchcocks with Grapes

2 spatchcocks (poussins), halved and backbones removed

30 g butter or margarine, melted

squeeze lemon juice

salt and pepper to taste

RED WINE SAUCE

backbones from birds

1 tablespoon vegetable oil

1 small onion, chopped

¼ cup (30 g) red grapes, seeded and chopped

¾ cup (180 ml) chicken stock

½ cup (125 ml) dry fruity red wine

¼ teaspoon thyme

½ small bay leaf

8 red grapes, halved and seeded

8 seedless green grapes, halved

2 teaspoons butter

1 teaspoon Dijon mustard

1 Brush spatchcocks with melted butter and lemon juice. Sprinkle with salt and pepper. Set aside.

2 To Prepare Sauce: Brown backbones in oil. Sauté onion and grapes lightly until light brown in colour.

3 Add chicken stock, wine, thyme and bay leaf. Bring to boil. Simmer to reduce to ⅔ cup. Strain stock. Cover. Chill.

4 Soften red and green grape halves in butter. Stir in reserved stock. Cook gently till reduced and slightly thickened. Whisk in mustard.

5 To Prepare Spatchcocks: Cook under a hot grill skin side down for 4 to 5 minutes, brushing frequently with remaining butter and lemon juice.

6 Turn, baste and grill a further 6 minutes. Longer time may be required depending on size of bird. Test with a skewer. Juices will run clear when cooked.

7 Serve the spatchcocks with a little sauce. Serve rest of sauce separately.

SERVES 4

STEP-BY-STEP TECHNIQUES

LEMON SOLE *with* GRAPES

1 whole lemon sole or silver dory, filleted and skinned

30 g butter or margarine

¼ cup (15 g) spring onions, chopped

1 bouquet garni

250 ml fish stock (see note)

salt and white pepper to taste

125 g sultana grapes

1 tablespoon Calvados or brandy

2 teaspoons flour

¼ cup (60 ml) dry white wine

¼ cup (60 ml) cream

1 Check fillets for bones. Roll up fillets, starting with tail end. Secure with kitchen string.

2 Melt half of butter in a heavy based frying pan with a lid. Add spring onions, reserving 2 tablespoons. Fry over a low heat until soft.

3 Add bouquet garni, fish stock and fish. Season. Simmer, covered, for 5 to 10 minutes or until the fish flakes when tested.

4 While fish is cooking, macerate grapes in Calvados for 15 minutes.

5 When fish is cooked, drain, remove string and keep warm on a serving dish. Strain cooking liquid, reserving ½ cup (125 ml).

6 In a clean pan, melt remaining butter. Sauté remaining spring onions until soft. Add flour. Cook, stirring, for 1 minute. Gradually add wine off the heat. Return to heat. Simmer until reduced by a quarter.

7 Add reserved stock. Bring to boil, then simmer for 5 minutes. Taste and adjust seasoning.

7 Stir in cream and grapes. Heat through gently. Pour over fish.

Lemon Sole with Grapes

Roll up fillets and tie securely with string

Place fillets in fish stock mixture and simmer gently until fish flakes when tested

To make sauce, add wine to cooked spring onions and simmer to reduce by a quarter

NOTE: Prepare fish stock by covering fish heads and bones with water. Add some chopped vegetables and a few peppercorns. Simmer for 20 minutes. Strain and use immediately. Do not store.

SERVES 4

Summer Fruit Meringue

SUMMER FRUIT MERINGUE

4 egg whites

1 cup (250 g) caster sugar

1 mango, peeled, seeded and sliced

2 kiwi fruit, peeled and sliced

KIWI FRUIT SAUCE

3 kiwi fruit, peeled and pureed

1 tablespoon icing sugar

juice ½ lemon

MANGO SAUCE

1 mango, peeled, seeded and pureed

1 tablespoon icing sugar

juice ½ lime

1 Whisk egg whites until stiff peaks form. Gradually add sugar, beating until dissolved. Line a baking tray with aluminium foil. Spoon meringue into the middle and smooth with spatula to make a 22 cm circle.

2 Using fork, fluff the sides to give an uneven texture, leaving a hollow in the middle.

3 Bake at 120°C (250°F) for 1¼ hours. Allow to cool in the oven with the door ajar. Peel away aluminium foil.

4 TO PREPARE KIWI FRUIT SAUCE: Purée kiwi fruit with icing sugar and juice. Pass through sieve to remove black seeds. Chill well.

5 TO PREPARE MANGO SAUCE: Purée mangoes with icing sugar and juice. Chill thoroughly.

6 Spoon Mango Sauce on half a 25 cm serving plate (with sides). Spoon the Kiwi Fruit Sauce onto the other half.

7 Place the meringue shell on top of sauce. Fill the hollow with fruit. Place mango slices on the same side as the Kiwi Fruit Sauce and the kiwi fruit slices on the Mango Sauce. Dust with icing sugar to serve.

SERVES 8

Kiwi Fruit *and* Mango Sorbet

6 kiwi fruit, peeled and sliced

1 ripe mango, peeled, stoned and sliced

1¼ cups (310 ml) sugar syrup (see note)

1 tablespoon orange juice

1 Purée the kiwi fruit and mango in a food processor. Add sugar syrup and orange juice. Blend well.

2 Pour mixture into freezing tray. Freeze 1 hour or until ice crystals form.

3 Remove. Process in food processor. Pour mixture back into tray. Freeze.

4 Just before serving, spoon into chilled glasses with extra slices of the 2 fruits for garnish.

NOTE: To make sugar syrup, dissolve 1 cup sugar in 1 cup water. Bring to boil. Remove from heat, cool. Store covered in refrigerator until needed.

SERVES 6

Passionfruit Mousse

2 eggs, separated

¼ cup (60 g) caster sugar

rind and juice of 1 lime or lemon

300 ml thickened cream, whipped

pulp of 4 passionfruit

1 Whisk egg yolks and sugar in a large bowl until thick and creamy. Add rind and juice. Mix well.

2 Fold in cream and passionfruit. Beat egg whites until soft peaks form. Lightly fold into cream mixture.

3 Spoon into serving dishes. Refrigerate until very cold. Serve with slices of fresh fruit or Passionfruit Sauce (recipe page 63).

SERVES 4 TO 6

COOK'S TIP

Always ensure that when whipping cream that it is cold or it may curdle.

TO PEEL KIWI FRUIT WITH EASE

Kiwi fruit are very easily peeled. Simply use a sharp knife to top and tail the fruit. With the tip of a knife, peel the skin away lengthwise.

Kiwi Fruit and Mango Sorbet

250 g black grapes
¼ cup (60 ml) brandy
1 egg white
¼ cup (60 g) sugar

1 Boil white wine and lemon rind 2 minutes. Blend yolks with ½ the sugar. Mix cornflour with water to form a smooth paste. Whisk into yolks. Gradually stir in hot wine.

2 Cook in top of double saucepan over simmering water until thick, stirring all the time. Remove from heat.

3 Whisk whites until stiff peaks form. Add remaining sugar gradually, beating until thick and glossy. Fold in warmed custard with lemon juice.

4 Reserve some grapes for decoration. Halve and seed remaining grapes. Soak in brandy.

5 Beat remaining egg white. Dip rims of 6 tall glasses first into beaten egg white, then into sugar. Dip reserved grapes into beaten egg white and sugar. Allow to dry. Chill.

6 Just before serving divide brandied grapes between glasses. Top up with custard mixture. Decorate with chilled frosted grapes.

SERVES 6

FIG *and* PASSIONFRUIT JAM

500 g figs, sliced
1 cup (250 g) passionfruit pulp
sugar

1 Boil figs and passionfruit together for 10 minutes. Measure and allow 1 cup sugar to each cup fruit.

2 Blend in sugar. Boil again until a little tested on a cold saucer wrinkles when touched.

3 Pour into warm, sterilised jars. Seal when cold.

MAKES ABOUT 3 CUPS

Grape and Wine Custard

GRAPE *and* WINE CUSTARD

THE FROSTING ON THE GRAPE

Simply dip grapes in lightly beaten egg white followed by caster sugar. Leave to dry on greaseproof paper.

1¼ cups (310 ml) sweet white wine
grated rind 1 lemon
4 eggs, separated
½ cup (125 g) caster sugar
2 tablespoons cornflour
3 tablespoons water
juice ½ lemon
250 g white muscat grapes

PASSIONFRUIT PUNCH

1 cup (250 g) sugar

½ cup (125 ml) water

1 cup (250 ml) orange juice

1 cup (250 ml) lemon juice

1 cup (125 g) passionfruit pulp

ice cubes

1 bottle sparkling white wine

orange and lemon slices for garnish

1 Bring sugar and water to the boil, stirring constantly. Continue to boil for 5 minutes. Allow to cool.

2 Add orange and lemon juices and passionfruit. Chill until needed.

3 To serve, place a quantity of ice cubes in punch bowl. Pour reserved syrup over ice. Mix in wine. Garnish with orange and lemon slices.

MAKES 1.5 LITRES

PASSIONA

1½ cups (375 ml) water

1½ cups (375 g) sugar

1½ teaspoons tartaric acid

pulp 48 passionfruit

1 Heat water, sugar and tartaric acid together, stirring, until sugar dissolves. Bring to the boil. Simmer 3 to 4 minutes.

2 While still boiling, add passionfruit, beating with a fork for 3 minutes to extract all the juice. Pour into bowl, mix well. Bottle.

3 To serve, add a small quantity to a glass of water or soda water. If well corked it will keep for some time.

MAKES 600 ML

PASSIONFRUIT SAUCE

½ cup (125 g) caster sugar

1 cup (250 ml) water

4 passionfruit

1 Dissolve sugar in water in a small saucepan over a low heat. Bring to the boil. Simmer until liquid has reduced by half. Stir in passionfruit pulp. Simmer for 2 minutes. Cool. Serve with desserts of choice or over ice cream.

MAKES ABOUT 1½ CUPS

BRANDIED GRAPE PRESERVE

1⅓ cups (330 ml) red wine vinegar

1½ cups (375 ml) red wine

¾ cup (180 g) sugar

3 cloves

4 sticks cinnamon

2 tablespoons brandy

1 kg black grapes, seeded

1 Bring vinegar, wine, sugar, cloves and cinnamon sticks to the boil. Simmer for 15 minutes or until syrupy.

2 Remove cinnamon sticks. Add brandy. Pour over grapes. Put into warm, sterilised jars. Seal.

NOTE: Serve with terrines, game birds and venison.

MAKES ABOUT 4 CUPS

TO PREPARE BOUQUET GARNI

A bouquet garni is a flavouring easily prepared by tying together herbs and celery studded with peppercorns. Add to dish during cooking. Alternatively, wrap herbs in muslin, or use the commercially-prepared variety.

MELONS

Nothing beats a slice of icy cold melon on a hot day. Their juicy sweetness leaves you ready for more. A melon's flesh is just about 95 per cent water, so is it any wonder that they are just as refreshing as a cool drink?

Melons come in lots of shapes and sizes, but the most popular ones here are watermelons, rockmelons and honeydew melons (although others are available).

Eat melons when they are perfectly ripe for optimum flavour. Aroma is a good way to test this – they usually taste like they smell!

Watermelons are more difficult to test for ripeness due to their thick skin. Choose those that are firm with even colouration. It is best to purchase a piece from a cut melon – look for firm, crisp, brightly coloured flesh and a soft waxy rind.

Melons keep well in the refrigerator. If unripe when purchased, leave at room temperature for a few days until ripe and then store in the refrigerator.

Melons are quite versatile and, due to their sweet, juicy flesh, complement many foods and flavourings. The recipes we have chosen for this section demonstrate this by teaming them with seafood, pastry and curry to name but a few.

TWO-MELON SUMMER SOUP

This soup looks beautiful served in glass bowls.

750 g rockmelon (cantaloupe)
2 tablespoons fresh lemon juice
2 ripe honeydew melons, 1 kg each
3 tablespoons fresh lime juice
2 teaspoons finely chopped fresh mint
mint sprigs for garnish
cream to serve if required

1 Halve rockmelon. Scoop out and discard the seeds. Peel and chop. Purée the rockmelon with the lemon juice in a food processor until smooth. Chill in a covered bowl for at least 12 hours.

2 Halve honeydew. Scoop out and discard the seeds. Peel and chop. Purée the honeydew melon with lime juice and mint in a food processor until smooth. Chill separately in a covered bowl for 12 hours.

3 To serve, place the purées into separate jugs. Pour at the same time, but from separate sides, into chilled serving bowls. The soup should stay in separate colours. Garnish with mint sprigs.

SERVES 6

MELON SHAPES

Melon flesh may be sliced, diced or cut into balls using a melon baller (which come in varying sizes).

HONEYDEW MELON *with* CRAB

2 honeydew melons, halved and seeded
185 g can crabmeat, drained and flaked
½ cup (125 ml) cream
½ cup (125 ml) mayonnaise
½ to 1 teaspoon curry powder
mint or parsley for garnish

1 Scoop all flesh from melons with a melon baller. Reserve shells.

2 Mix remaining ingredients together. Combine with melon balls.

3 Spoon into melon halves. Garnish with mint or parsley. Chill thoroughly before serving.

SERVES 4

WATERMELON SOUP

2 kg watermelon flesh, seeded
2 cups (500 ml) sweet white wine
3 tablespoons honey
½ teaspoon garam masala
grated rind and juice 1 orange
graded rind 1 lemon
1 cup (250 ml) sour cream
grated nutmeg and dill sprigs for garnish

1 Bring watermelon, wine, honey, garam masala, orange rind and juice and lemon rind to the boil, stirring constantly. Reduce heat. Simmer for 20 minutes. Allow to cool.

2 Purée in blender or food processor. Transfer to a bowl. Stir in sour cream. Chill thoroughly before serving.

3 Serve garnished with dill sprigs and a light sprinkling of grated nutmeg.

SERVES 6

A SERVING SUGGESTION

Melon skins, once hollowed out, make useful serving containers for salads, sorbet, ice cream etc.

THIRST QUENCHERS

Melons make delicious drinks when processed.

Two-melon Summer Soup

ROCKMELON SOUP

750 g rockmelon (cantaloupe), halved and seeded

200 g seedless grapes

200 g apricots, halved and stoned

1 apple, peeled, cored and sliced

3 cups (750 ml) dry white wine

2 to 3 tablespoons lemon juice

1½ teaspoons cornflour

1 tablespoon honey

¼ cup (30 g) pinenuts

1 Remove flesh from half the rockmelon and chop. Scoop flesh from remaining half into balls using a melon baller.

2 Simmer chopped melon, grapes, apricots, apple, wine and lemon juice for 20 minutes. Allow to cool. Purée in a food processor.

3 Return purée to saucepan. Blend cornflour with a little water to form a smooth paste. Stir cornflour and honey into soup. Bring to the boil, stirring constantly. Simmer for 3 minutes

4 Stir in melon balls. Chill thoroughly. Toast pinenuts by tossing in a dry frying pan over a low heat until golden. Nuts may also be toasted by spreading in a single layer on a baking tray and baking in a slow oven 150°C (300°F) until golden. Sprinkle over soup when serving.

Rockmelon Soup

SERVES 6

SPICY MELON SALAD

If you really need to prepare the salad in advance, cut the avocado and toss in a little lemon juice to help prevent browning.

½ rockmelon (cantaloupe), balled or sliced

½ honeydew melon, balled or sliced

1 cup (125 g) watermelon dice

3 shallots, chopped

125 g prosciutto, cut into strips

1 avocado, sliced

¼ cup (30 g) sliced sundried tomatoes

DRESSING

¼ cup (60 ml) olive oil

2 tablespoons white wine vinegar

1 teaspoon curry powder

few drops chilli sauce

seasonings to taste

1 Arrange all ingredients for salad on a shallow serving platter or individual serving plates (see note).

2 TO PREPARE DRESSING: Combine all ingredients in a screwtop jar. Shake well. Pour over salad just before serving. Serve as an entree, or light lunch.

SERVES 6 TO 8

Simmer fruit, lemon juice and wine for 20 minutes

Cool, then purée mixture using a sieve or in a food processor

Add cornflour mixture and honey to purée and cook until slightly thickened

POACHED SCALLOPS *with* MELON, MANGO *and* SNOW PEAS *in* SESAME DILL DRESSING

12 uncooked fresh scallops

30 g pickled ginger, chopped

2 tablespoons dry white wine

1 small honeydew or rockmelon (cantaloupe), scooped into balls with a melon baller

1 mango, peeled and thinly sliced

100 g snow peas, blanched and chopped

6 cherry tomatoes, halved

4 asparagus spears, halved lengthways and cooked

SESAME DILL DRESSING

juice 1 lemon

2 teaspoons chopped dill

3 to 4 drops sesame oil

vegetable oil

salt and freshly ground pepper, to taste

1 Combine scallops and ginger and allow to stand for 20 minutes.

2 Heat wine. Blanch scallops and ginger in wine for 1 minute. Drain to remove all pickling solution. Cool.

3 Toss all ingredients except asparagus in Sesame Dill Dressing. Arrange the salad ingredients on 4 chilled plates. Garnish with asparagus spears.

4 TO PREPARE SESAME DILL DRESSING: Combine lemon juice, dill and sesame oil in a measuring cup. Top with oil to bring up to 150 ml. Season. Pour into a screwtop jar. Shake well.

SERVES 4

TO MICROWAVE ASPARAGUS

To cook asparagus: Rinse well. Place in a shallow microwave safe dish. Cover with plastic wrap. Cook on HIGH (100%) for 1 minute or until tender.

STEP-BY-STEP TECHNIQUES

Add chopped ginger to mixture of coriander seeds, curry powder, onion and flour

Slowly blend in then bring to boil

Stir in coconut, mixed fruits and cream

FRUIT CURRY

4 to 5 pieces crystallised ginger

2 onions, peeled and chopped

60 g butter or margarine

1 tablespoon curry powder

1 tablespoon plain flour

1 teaspoon crushed coriander seeds

2 cups (500 ml) chicken stock

2 teaspoons lemon juice

salt and freshly ground black pepper

3 cups (270 g) desiccated coconut

4 to 5 cups (500 g-625 g) chopped mixed fruits (melons, peaches, plums, grapes, bananas, apples, pears)

2 to 3 tablespoons cream

1 Cover ginger with hot water for a few minutes to remove sugar. Drain. Pat dry. Chop finely.

2 Fry onions in butter until tender. Stir in curry powder, flour and coriander seeds and ginger. Cook gently for 5 minutes.

3 Gradually blend in stock. Bring to boil. Stir in lemon juice and seasonings. Simmer for 30 minutes.

4 Stir in coconut, prepared fruits and cream. Serve hot or cold with rice.

SERVES 4

Fruit Curry

Fruit Flan

Pastry Bases
4 sheets ready rolled shortcrust pastry

1 egg, beaten

Filling
500 g cream cheese, softened

1 cup (250 g) caster sugar

1 teaspoon cinnamon

juice and grated rind of a lemon

Topping
1 honeydew melon, seeded and scooped into balls

300 g black grapes, stems removed

½ rockmelon (cantaloupe), seeded and scooped into balls

2 punnets strawberries, hulled

2 kiwi fruit, peeled and sliced

Glaze
1 cup apricot jam, warmed and sieved

½ cup orange juice or water

1 Preheat oven to 200°C (400°F). Join 2 pastry sheets together, pressing join firmly. Repeat with remaining 2 sheets.

2 Lightly grease 2 x 23 cm flan tins. Press pastry gently into base. Bake blind (see note) for 10 minutes.

3 Remove baking beans. Prick pastry base with fork. Cool completely before filling. Do not fill more than 3 hours before serving.

4 To Prepare Filling: Combine filling ingredients until smooth and creamy. Spoon equal amounts into the flan cases. Smooth top of each with a spatula. Refrigerate until firm (about 1 hour).

5 Top decoratively with prepared fruit.

6 To Prepare Glaze: Combine ingredients. Lightly brush over fruit. Chill before serving.

Fruit Flan

❦ To Bake Blind

Cover pastry with a piece of baking paper. Cover with dried beans, peas, rice or pasta. Bake according to instructions. Remove paper and beans. Continue as directed.

FRESH
from the
TROPICS

Many fruit can be classified as tropical and in this section we have included fruits such as pineapple, bananas, mango, pawpaw, lychees and other exotic, less well-known fruit, grown in hot climates. These fruits are mostly soft fleshed and are delicious in mousse, ice cream, sorbet and jelly.

Mangoes are a favourite of many – with good reason, as they are one of the most delicious tropical fruits. They are still fairly expensive, but one taste of that sweet, juicy flesh, makes the cost worthwhile. Select those with shiny, unblemished skins that if squeezed gently will give slightly. They will ripen in a warm room and keep well if refrigerated.

Pineapples are another very popular tropical fruit which grow straight out of the ground. They are sweet, aromatic and acidic all at once which makes them delicious in salads or even as an accompaniment to pork or ham.

The oriental fruit lychee and its relative the rambutan are best served whole to really appreciate their flavour. In this chapter we have some lovely serving suggestions for these fruit.

TANGY MANGO *and* CUCUMBER SOUP

3 spring onions, chopped
1 mango, peeled, seeded and puréed
½ cup (125 ml) lemon juice
½ cup (125 ml) orange and mango juice
½ cup (125 ml) natural low-fat yoghurt
1 clove garlic, crushed
1½ cucumbers, peeled, seeded and grated
salt and freshly ground pepper, to taste
½ red capsicum (pepper), finely diced

1 Place spring onions, mango, lemon juice, orange and mango juice, yoghurt and garlic in a food processor or blender. Process until smooth. Transfer to a serving bowl. Add grated cucumber and seasonings.
2 Chill until ready to serve. Garnish with sliced cucumber and finely diced capsicum.

SERVES 4

CUSTARD APPLE SOUP

2 medium-size, ripe custard apples
2 cups (500 ml) chicken stock
juice 2 limes
1 cup (250 ml) sour cream
salt and freshly ground pepper, to taste
lemon slices and dill sprigs for garnish

1 Scoop out flesh of custard apples, discarding seeds. Purée in blender or food processor, gradually adding stock, until smooth. Blend in lime juice.
2 Transfer mixture to bowl. Stir in sour cream and seasonings. Serve in bowls garnished with lemon slices and dill.

SERVES 4

MILD CURRY *and* MANGO SOUP

1 mango, peeled and flesh removed or 450 g can mango slices
2 cups chicken stock
juice ½ lemon
¼ teaspoon curry powder
salt and freshly ground pepper, to taste
½ cup (125 ml) cream
1 teaspoon saffron threads

1 Place mango, stock and lemon juice in a food processor or blender. Process until smooth.
2 Add curry powder and seasonings. Gently heat soup until hot. Do not allow to boil. Stir in cream before serving.
3 If serving cold there is no need to cook the soup, just purée with the seasoning and cream.
4 Serve with croutons or crusty bread and garnish with a few saffron threads.

SERVES 4

LYCHEE COCKTAIL

250 g lychees or rambutans, peeled, halved and seeded
1 cup (200 g) diced pineapple
1 cup (150 g) diced orange
1 tablespoon sugar
2 teaspoons lemon juice

1 Combine fruits. Chill for 1 hour. Add sugar and lemon juice. Serve in chilled cocktail glasses.

SERVES 4

PIZZA SUPREME

1 teaspoon caster sugar

⅓ cup (160 ml) warm water

1 teaspoon dry yeast

½ cup (60 g) wholemeal flour

½ cup (60 g) plain flour

2 teaspoons butter

2 teaspoons oil

TOPPING

3 tablespoons tomato paste

1 tomato, sliced

1 onion, sliced

60 g mushrooms, sliced

60 g salami, sliced

3 slices pineapple, chopped

12 black olives

6 anchovy fillets

250 g mozzarella cheese, sliced

1 Dissolve sugar in water. Stir in yeast. Set aside until frothy. Mix together flours. Rub in butter.

2 Add yeast, liquid and oil. Mix until sides of bowl are clean.

3 Knead dough on lightly floured surface. Clean bowl. Lightly oil it and leave dough in it, covered, to rise until double in size.

4 Knock back dough. Knead until smooth. Pat dough into a 23 cm pizza tray. Brush with oil. Leave for 15 minutes before baking.

5 TO PREPARE TOPPING: Spread base with tomato paste. Arrange other topping ingredients over paste. Bake at 200°C (400°F) for 25 to 30 minutes.

MAKES 1 PIZZA

PERFECT PINEAPPLE PIECES

After peeling pineapples, make sure all of the hard, unpalatable 'eyes' are removed before serving.

Pizza Supreme

Racks of Lamb with Parsley Mint Crust

RACKS of LAMB with PARSLEY MINT CRUST

60 g butter or margarine

1 tablespoon mango chutney

2 teaspoons French mustard

1 clove garlic, crushed

2 teaspoons lemon juice

6 racks lamb (3 chops each), excess fat trimmed

6 tablespoons finely chopped fresh parsley

2 tablespoons finely chopped fresh mint

salt and freshly ground black pepper

MANGO MINT SAUCE

1 mango, peeled, seeded and pureed

1 tablespoon finely chopped fresh mint

freshly ground black pepper

1 teaspoon vinegar

1 Combine butter, chutney, mustard, garlic and lemon juice. Spread evenly over the back of each lamb rack.

2 Sprinkle over parsley, mint and seasonings. Press on to lamb using the back of a metal spoon.

3 Bake at 200°C (400°F) for 20 to 30 minutes or until tender.

4 **TO PREPARE SAUCE:** Combine ingredients in a small saucepan. Heat gently then serve.

SERVES 6

Pork Salad *with* Ginger Mango Dressing

1 lettuce, washed and drained

600 g pork fillet, fried and sliced into medallions

½ pineapple, peeled and chopped

4 stalks celery, sliced

100 g hazelnuts, toasted

100 g mushrooms

1 mango, peeled, seeded and chopped or 450 g can mango slices

1 red apple, sliced and sprinkled with lemon juice to prevent browning

salt and freshly ground pepper, to taste

snipped chives

GINGER MANGO DRESSING

2 mangoes, peeled and seeded

⅔ cup (160 g) mayonnaise

1 teaspoon ginger

1 Tear lettuce leaves into bite-sized pieces, reserving a few large leaves to line salad bowl. Mix together remaining ingredients, except chives. Spoon into serving bowl.

2 TO PREPARE GINGER MANGO DRESSING: Purée mango, mayonnaise and ginger until smooth.

3 Toss through dressing. Garnish with chives. Serve.

SERVES 4 TO 6

PEELING LYCHEES AND RAMBUTANS

When using fresh lychees, peel by breaking open the skin and pressing. The fruit will pop out. Rambutans only require peeling with a knife.

Pork Salad with Ginger Mango Dressing

STIR-FRIED MANGO CHICKEN *with* ALMONDS

**3 chicken breasts, skinned, boned and cut
into thin strips**

**1 tablespoon cornflour mixed with
1 tablespoon light soy sauce and
2 tablespoons sherry**

6 tablespoons oil

1½ teaspoons chopped ginger root

1 clove garlic, crushed

**4 spring onions, white part chopped and
green part cut into 2.5 cm pieces**

salt and freshly ground pepper

2 mangoes, peeled and cut in long strips

2 tablespoons sherry

1 tablespoon light soy sauce

1 teaspoon brown sugar

1 teaspoon cornflour

½ cup (125 g) slivered almonds, toasted

1 Place chicken in a bowl. Spoon cornflour mixture over chicken strips. Marinate in the refrigerator for 30 minutes. Drain.

2 Heat 3 tablespoons oil in a wok over high heat. Stir-fry chicken for 30 seconds. Remove. Drain on absorbent paper.

3 Heat 2 tablespoons oil and stir-fry ginger, garlic, white part of the spring onions and seasonings for 30 seconds.

4 Reheat chicken in the wok for 1 minute. Place chicken in a serving dish.

5 Heat 1 tablespoon of oil in the wok. Add mangoes. Stir-fry for 30 seconds. Stir in sherry, soy sauce, sugar and cornflour. Cook 30 seconds or until the sauce thickens.

6 Add the green spring onions pieces and almonds. Pour over chicken. Garnish with sliced spring onions.

SERVES 4

*Stir-fried Mango
Chicken with Almonds*

VEAL *with* POMEGRANATES

1 teaspoon salt

freshly ground black pepper

1 teaspoon paprika

¼ teaspoon allspice

¼ cup (30 g) plain flour

1 kg stewing veal, cut in 2.5 cm dice

¼ cup (60 ml) oil

1 large onion, peeled and chopped

1 cup (250 ml) veal or chicken stock

1 tablespoon tomato paste

juice 3 large pomegranates

1 tablespoon honey

½ cup (30 g) chopped celery

½ red capsicum (pepper), seeded, thinly sliced

pomegranate seeds and parsley for garnish

1 Mix salt, pepper, paprika and allspice with flour. Dust diced veal with flour. Shake off excess.

2 Brown veal in oil. Transfer to casserole. Saute onion in same pan. Add stock, tomato paste, pomegranate juice and honey. Mix well.

3 Pour sauce over veal. Bake, covered, at 150°C (300°F) for 1 hour 45 minutes. Add celery and capsicum. Cook a further 15 minutes or until meat is tender. Garnish with pomegranate seeds and parsley.

NOTE: To make pomegranate juice, cut ripe pomegranates in half and squeeze on lemon juicer to crush seeds.

SERVES 6

FISH *and* FRUIT SALAD

500 g white fish fillets

¼ cup (60 ml) lemon juice

6 guavas, stoned and diced

3 slices fresh pineapple, diced

3 bananas, sliced

1 large firm ripe mango, peeled, stoned and diced

1 Spanish onion, thinly sliced

1 red chilli, seeded and finely chopped

¾ cup (180 ml) thick coconut milk

red capsicum or snipped chives for garnish

1 Cut fish into narrow strips. Marinate in lemon juice for at least 6 hours. Drain.

2 Arrange the fish and prepared fruit in a salad bowl. Garnish with the onion and chilli. Pour over coconut milk. Chill thoroughly.

3 Garnish with strips of red capsicum or chives. Coconut milk may be served separately if preferred.

SERVES 4

STORING BANANAS

Always store bananas at room temperature. Never refrigerate or freeze them as they will turn black.

Veal with Pomegranates

Coat diced veal with seasoned flour

Brown veal in oil

Pour pomegranate sauce over veal

4 Whip cream. Fold into mixture. Pour into a greased 23 cm ring mould. Leave to set in refrigerator for 3 to 4 hours.

5 Turn pudding on to serving dish. Scoop out flesh from pawpaw with melon baller. Pile in centre of pudding. Garnish with lime slices.

NOTE: When grating rind from lemon or orange, do so gently as only the colour is wanted. The white pith is bitter.

SERVES 6

Smoked Turkey with Pawpaw

SUN GLORY PAWPAW PUDDING

If pawpaw is not available, substitute any melon.

300 ml milk

⅓ cup (60 g) semolina

2 tablespoons gelatine

2 tablespoons honey

juice and grated rind 1 lemon

juice and grated rind 1 orange

1 cup (125 g) pawpaw pulp

150 ml cream

1 pawpaw

2 limes or lemons, thinly sliced

1 Bring milk to the boil. Stir in semolina. Cook 5 minutes.

2 Blend gelatine and honey. Stir into hot semolina mixture until dissolved.

3 Flavour with lemon and orange rind and juice. Stir in pawpaw. Cool.

EASY PAWPAWS

Pawpaw are delicious soaked in lime or orange juice.

SMOKED TURKEY *with* PAWPAW

Prosciutto can be used instead of turkey for a different flavour.

1 medium-sized pawpaw

12 thin slices smoked turkey breast

lime wedges and watercress sprigs, to garnish

CRANBERRY MAYONNAISE

½ cup (125 ml) mayonnaise

3 tablespoons cranberry sauce

1 Peel, halve and remove seeds from pawpaw. Cut each half lengthways into thirds.

2 Arrange 2 thin slices of turkey on each portion of pawpaw. Serve on individual plates, garnished with lime wedges, watercress sprigs and Cranberry Mayonnaise.

3 TO PREPARE CRANBERRY MAYONNAISE: Blend ingredients together well.

SERVES 6

MANGO *and* PRAWN SALAD

12 prawns, shelled and deveined

2 mangoes, peeled

125 g snow peas

4 spring onions, chopped

1 cup (125 g) pecans

salt and freshly ground pepper

2 tablespoons French dressing

Make a small cut to expose vein on tail

Pull vein through

1 Halve prawns if large. Cut a large slice from each side of the mango stone, then cut away the remaining flesh. Cut the large mango slices into strips.

2 Blanch snow peas in boiling water for 1 minute. Drain. Cool under cold running water. If preferred snow peas can be served raw in the salad.

3 Combine prawns, mango, snow peas, shallots, pecans and seasonings. Pour over French dressing. Toss well before serving.

SERVES 4 TO 6

Mango and Prawn Salad

GINGER MANGO CHEESECAKE

CRUST

2½ cups (250 g) chocolate biscuit crumbs

125 g butter or margarine, melted

FILLING

¼ cup (60 ml) water

¼ cup (60 ml) lemon juice

25 g packet lemon jelly crystals

375 g can evaporated milk, chilled

200 g soft cream cheese

2 mangoes, peeled, seeded and roughly chopped or 2 x 450 g cans mango slices

¼ cup (45 g) brown sugar

1 teaspoon vanilla essence

1 tablespoon glace ginger, finely chopped

1 mango, sliced

whipped cream

Mango Ice Cream

½ lemon, thinly sliced and cut into small pieces

chocolate curls

1 TO PREPARE CRUST: Combine biscuit crumbs and melted butter thoroughly. Press into the bottom and sides of a greased 23 cm spring-form pan. Chill.

2 TO PREPARE FILLING: Heat water and lemon juice until boiling. Add jelly crystals. Stir to dissolve. Allow to cool.

3 Whip evaporated milk until thick. Add cream cheese and mangoes. Beat until smooth. Blend in sugar, vanilla, ginger and jelly mixture. Pour over crumb crust. Chill.

4 Decorate with mango slices, cream, lemon slices and chocolate curls.

SERVES 10 TO 12

MANGO ICE CREAM

1 mango, peeled, seeded and roughly chopped

1 pawpaw, peeled, seeded and roughly chopped

1 tablespoon lemon juice

4 egg yolks

⅔ cup (125 g) icing sugar

¾ cup (180 ml) thickened cream, whipped

1 Purée mango and pawpaw together with lemon juice in a food processor. Set aside.

2 Combine egg yolks and icing sugar in the top of a double boiler. Whisk mixture until eggs are pale in colour and thick. Remove from heat. Whisk a further 2 minutes.

3 Fold the fruit purée gently into the egg mixture. Blend in cream.

4 Pour into decorative 1 litre metal mould. Freeze for a minimum of 3 hours.

5 To remove, dip the mould in warm water for 30 seconds. Turn out onto a serving platter or scoop out as ice cream balls.

NOTE: Canned mangoes can also be used in this recipe.

SERVES 6 TO 8

Tropical Sorbet

TROPICAL SORBET

MANGO SORBET
2 mangoes, peeled, seeded and puréed

1¼ cups (310 ml) water

⅔ cup (160 g) caster sugar

KIWI FRUIT SORBET
4 kiwi fruit, peeled and puréed

1¾ cups (435 ml) water

1 cup (250 g) caster sugar

juice and grated rind 1 lemon

PINEAPPLE SORBET
1¾ cups (435 ml) pineapple juice

⅔ cup (160 ml) water

⅔ cup (160 g) caster sugar

2 to 3 drops orange essence

fresh mint, to garnish

1 Spoon the 2 fruit purées and the pineapple juice into 3 separate bowls. Set aside.

2 TO PREPARE SUGAR SYRUPS: Place water and the required amounts of sugar into 3 separate saucepans. Stir until sugar dissolves.

3 Boil syrups for Mango and Kiwi Fruit Sorbets for 5 minutes. Boil syrup for Pineapple Sorbet for 3 minutes. Cool syrups. Add to their respective purées, and blend.

4 Add lemon juice and rind to Kiwi Fruit Sorbet and orange essence to Pineapple Sorbet.

5 Pour each mixture into separate freezer trays. Freeze for 2½ hours. Remove from freezer. Blend to break up the ice crystals. Return to freezer until frozen.

6 Allow sorbets to soften for 10 minutes at room temperature before serving. Place scoops of sorbet on chilled trays. Return to the freezer for 30 minutes to harden.

7 Arrange the sorbet scoops colourfully on individual serving plates. Garnish with mint.

SERVES 4 TO 6

TROPICAL FRUIT CAKE

3 cups (750 ml) water

1½ cups (375 g) sugar

4 small mangoes, peeled, seeded and diced

600 g pineapple, peeled, cored and diced

600 g cherries, stalks and pips removed

4 cups (500 g) plain flour

25 g fresh yeast or 1½ x 7 g sachet dry yeast

1 cup (250 ml) warm milk

125 g butter or margarine, cut into small pieces

3½ tablespoons sugar

3 tablespoons ground hazelnuts

1 teaspoon vanilla essence

salt to taste

TOPPING

2 cups (250 g) plain flour

1¼ cups (240 g) brown sugar

1½ teaspoons cinnamon

150 g butter or margarine, melted

1 Combine water and sugar in a saucepan. Stir until sugar is dissolved. Bring to boil. Boil, without stirring, for 10 minutes.

2 Remove pan from the heat. Add mangoes, pineapple and cherries to liquid for 5 minutes each. Remove.

Tropical Fruit Cake

Line tray with dough, forming a lip

Place cherries in a diagonal row

Arrange other fruits decoratively

A delicious alternative to a traditional Christmas Cake

3 Sift flour into bowl. Make a well in the centre. Dissolve the yeast in milk with 1 teaspoon sugar. Pour into the well. Mix together to form a dough. At this stage the dough will look very dry.

4 Lightly oil a clean bowl. Place dough in bowl. Leave to rise in a warm place until doubled in size.

5 When the dough has risen sufficiently, add butter, sugar, hazelnuts and vanilla. Work together until dough is smooth and elastic. Place in a lightly greased bowl. Leave to rise in a warm place for about 30 minutes. Knead the dough for 5 minutes. Roll out so it is big enough to fit a greased lamington tray. Turn the sides over to form a lip. Cover the dough with the fruits in 3 sections.

6 To Prepare Topping: Combine the flour, sugar, cinnamon and butter in a bowl. Rub together with fingers to form crumbs.

7 Sprinkle the crumble mixture evenly over fruit. Bake at 200°C (400°F) for 35 to 40 minutes.

Makes 24 pieces

Banana Soufflé

60 g butter or margarine

3 tablespoons flour

½ teaspoon vanilla essence

½ cup (125 ml) cream

2 ripe medium bananas

3 tablespoons caster sugar

4 eggs, separated

1 tablespoon desiccated coconut

1 Collar and lightly grease 4 individual 1 cup soufflé dishes. Dust with caster sugar.

2 Melt butter in a small saucepan. Stir in flour. Cook 1 minute. Remove from heat. Add vanilla and cream. Beat until smooth. Return to heat. Cook, stirring constantly, until sauce boils and thickens. Place sauce in a bowl. Allow to cool.

3 Mash bananas. Beat caster sugar, egg yolks and sauce into cooled mixture. Combine well.

4 Beat egg whites until stiff peaks form. Gently fold egg whites through banana mixture. Spoon mixture into prepared dishes. Sprinkle each with a little coconut.

5 Bake at 190°C (375°F) for 15 to 20 minutes. Serve immediately with whipped cream.

Serves 4

Banana Apricot Bread

1 cup (125 g) chopped dried apricots

¼ cup (60 ml) sherry

1¼ cups (150 g) flour

2 teaspoons baking powder

½ teaspoon bicarbonate of soda

90 g butter or margarine

grated rind 1 lemon

⅔ cup (160 g) caster sugar

2 eggs

½ cup (125 g) mashed banana

1 Soak apricots in sherry for 1 hour. Drain and discard sherry. Sift flour, baking powder and bicarbonate of soda twice. Set aside.

2 Cream butter, lemon rind and sugar together. Beat in eggs one at a time. Beat well after each addition. Fold in fruits alternately with flour mixture.

3 Place mixture into a greased and lined 10 x 20 cm loaf tin. Bake at 180°C (350°F) for 1 hour or until cooked.

4 Cool on wire rack. Ice if desired, with icing of your choice.

Makes 1 loaf

PEELING BANANAS

Once peeled or cut, bananas should be tossed in lemon juice to prevent them from going brown.

COOKING BANANAS

Bananas may be cooked in their skin either boiled, baked or grilled.

STEP-BY-STEP TECHNIQUES

PINEAPPLE SORBET

1 medium pineapple

2 limes

400 ml water

¾ cup (180 g) caster sugar

mint sprigs for garnish

1 Cut pineapple in half lengthwise, leaving leaves intact. Using grapefruit knife, remove the flesh, leaving shells whole for serving. Place pineapple shells in refrigerator until needed.

2 Peel limes, removing white pith. Cut in quarters. Purée lime and pineapple fruits in food processor.

3 Heat water and sugar, stirring until sugar dissolves. Simmer for 8 to 10 minutes until a thin syrup forms. Allow to cool. Add to pineapple mixture.

4 Pour into freezer trays. Freeze until set. Process again in food processor to break up ice crystals. Pour back into freezer trays. Cover with foil. Allow to refreeze.

5 When ready to serve, dip bottom of trays in hot water. Tip out sorbet. Cut into large dice. Pile sorbet into pineapple shells. Serve garnished with mint sprigs.

SERVES 6

Pineapple Sorbet

Remove flesh using a grapefruit knife

Peel limes and cut into quarters

Pour syrup into puréed fruit

Hot Mango *and* Tomato Chutney

6 under-ripe tomatoes, sliced

4 medium firm under-ripe mangoes, peeled,
seeded and diced

2 onions, peeled and chopped

2 cloves garlic, minced

1 cm piece ginger root, finely grated

1 cup (150 g) currants

4 red chillies, seeded and sliced

2 tablespoons chopped fresh coriander

¼ teaspoon cayenne pepper

2 cups (500 ml) malt vinegar

2 cups (300 g) brown sugar

1 teaspoon salt, optional

1 Place all ingredients in a heavy-based saucepan. Mix well. Bring to boil, then simmer gently for 10 minutes.

2 Reduce heat to low. Cook, stirring, until mangoes are soft and mixture is a jam-like consistency.

3 Remove from heat. Cool slightly. Bottle chutney in sterilised jars. Remove any air bubbles by piercing mixture with a skewer.

4 Cut out circles of greaseproof paper according to jar size. Place these on top of the chutney. Press lightly with fingertips to remove air.

5 Seal with sterilised lids. Store in a cool place. Refrigerate after opening.

MAKES ABOUT 1½ LITRES

Spicy Mango Sauce

2 mangoes, peeled, seeded and pureed

1 tablespoon Madeira

60 g butter or margarine

2 green chillies, finely chopped

1 teaspoon caraway seeds

salt and freshly ground pepper, to taste

1 Combine mango and Madeira until smooth. Melt butter in a small frying pan. Add all ingredients. Simmer, covered, for 8 minutes, stirring occasionally.

2 If sauce becomes too thick, thin with a little water. Store covered in refrigerator. Serve hot or cold with beef, pork, fish, chicken and rice dishes.

MAKES ABOUT 1½ CUPS

Hot Mango and Tomato Chutney

Persimmon Jam

Cut cross in pointed end of persimmon and peel back skin

Cook persimmon pulp and sugar over a low heat

Stir in lemon juice, rind and pineapple

PERSIMMON JAM

4 ripe persimmons

2 cups (500 g) sugar

½ cup (100 g) grated pineapple

1 tablespoon lemon juice

shredded peel 1 lemon

1 Cut a cross in pointed ends of persimmons. Peel back skin. Discard skin and stem end.

2 Combine persimmon pulp with sugar. Cook over low heat 15 minutes, stirring constantly until thickened and clear. Do not boil.

3 Stir in pineapple, lemon juice and rind. Pour into warm, sterilised jars. Seal when cool.

MAKES ABOUT 1½ CUPS

MANGO MINT COOLER

1 mango, peeled, seeded and puréed

½ cup (125 ml) orange and mango juice

½ cup (125 ml) lemonade

3 tablespoons Advocaat

2 tablespoons Crème de Menthe

mint leaves, to garnish

1 Combine all ingredients. Blend until smooth. Pour into tall glasses over ice. Garnish with mint leaves.

SERVES 2

TAMARILLO CHUTNEY

500 g brown sugar

250 g apples, peeled, cored and thinly sliced

250 g onion, peeled and finely chopped

12 tamarillos, blanched and diced

300 ml white vinegar

2 teaspoons mixed spice

2 teaspoons salt

pinch cayenne pepper

1 Place all ingredients in a saucepan and bring to the boil. Reduce heat. Simmer for 45 minutes or until thick, stirring occasionally.

2 Pour into warm, sterilised jars. Seal.

MAKES ABOUT 4 CUPS

FEIJOA *and* GUAVA JELLY

1.25 kg feijoas

1 kg apples, cored

500 g guavas

sugar

1 Cut up all fruit roughly. Cover with water. Boil for 1 hour or until mushy.

2 Push through a sieve, or strain through a jelly bag or muslin overnight.

3 Measure juice. Allow ¾ cup (180 g) sugar to each cup of juice. Bring juice to the boil, add sugar, stirring until dissolved.

4 Boil rapidly for 10 minutes or until a few drops tested on a cold saucer wrinkles when touched.

5 Pour into warm, sterilised jars. Seal when cold.

MAKES ABOUT 6 CUPS

Feijoa and Guava Jelly

Cut up fruit roughly

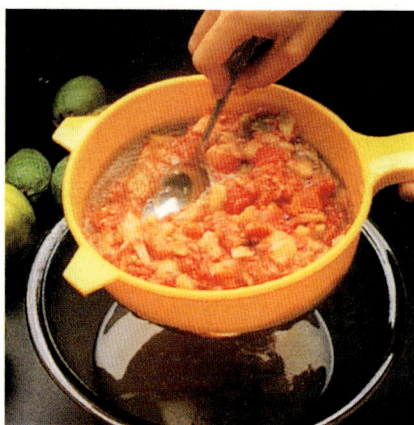

Press cooked fruit through sieve

Bring juice to the boil and add sugar

PICK OF THE CROP

PRODUCE	SOUTHERN HEMISPHERE	NORTHERN HEMISPHERE
Apples (Delicious)	All year	All year
Apples (Red) (Jonathon, Rome, Beauty, Bonza)	March to December	October to March
Apples (Green) (Granny Smith)	All year	All year
Apricots	November to February	June to August
Avocadoes (Alligator Pears)	All year	All year
Bananas	All year	All year
Cherries	October to mid January	May to July
Custard Apple	April to August	June to December
Carambola (Star Fruit)	October to July	June to July
Coconuts	All year	All year
Dates	All year	All year
Feijoas	May to August	All year

PRODUCE	SOUTHERN HEMISPHERE	NORTHERN HEMISPHERE
Figs, Fresh	December to May	July to September
Grapefruit	All year	All year
Grapes (Early Varieties)	November	All year
Grapes (Black Muscat)	December to April	July to May
Grapes (White/Black Varieties)	January to June	All year
Grapes (Sultanas)	January to May	June to July / January to February
Guava	November to May	All year
Honeydew	All year	February to December
Kiwi Fruit (Chinese Gooseberry)	All year	All year
Lemons	All year	All year
Limes	June to September	All year
Lychees (Litchis)	November to March	December to March
Mandarins (Clementines, Tangerines, Satsuma)	April to October	July to February

PRODUCE	SOUTHERN HEMISPHERE	NORTHERN HEMISPHERE
Mangoes	November to March	All year
Oranges (Navels)	May to October	November to March / May to July
Oranges (Valencia)	September to April	April to November
Pawpaw (Papaya)	All year	All year
Passionfruit (Purple Granadilla)	All year	All year
Peaches	November to March	May to September / December to January
Pears	All year	All year
Persimmons (Kaki Fruit, Sharon Fruit, Apple of the Orient)	February to June	October to December
Pineapples	All year	All year
Plums (Early Varieties)	December	July to April
Plums (Wilsons)	November to December	July to April
Plums (Blood & others)	December to February	July to April
Plums (President)	March to May	July to April

PRODUCE	SOUTHERN HEMISPHERE	NORTHERN HEMISPHERE
Quinces (Japonicas)	January to May	Mid July
Rhubarb	All year	January to September
Rockmelon	All year	July to September
Strawberries	All year	June to July
Strawberries (Imported)	May to July	All year
Rambutans	September to May	All year
Tamarillo	March to December	August to September
Watermelon	All year	May to September
Boysenberries	December to February	July to August
Redcurrants, Blackcurrants	December	June to September
Mulberries	October to December	June to September
Blackberries	January to March	August to September
Gooseberries	October to February	June to July
Raspberries	November to February	July to August

MEASURING MADE EASY

HOW TO MEASURE LIQUIDS

METRIC	IMPERIAL	CUPS
30 ml	1 fluid ounce	1 tablespoon plus 2 teaspoons
60 ml	2 fluid ounces	¼ cup
90 ml	3 fluid ounces	
125 ml	4 fluid ounces	½ cup
150 ml	5 fluid ounces	
170 ml	5 ½ fluid ounces	
180 ml	6 fluid ounces	¾ cup
220 ml	7 fluid ounces	
250 ml	8 fluid ounces	1 cup
500 ml	16 fluid ounces	2 cups
600 ml	20 fluid ounces (1 pint)	2 ½ cups
1 litre	1 ¾ pints	

HOW TO MEASURE DRY INGREDIENTS

15 g	1/2 oz	
30 g	1 oz	
60 g	2 oz	
90 g	3 oz	
125 g	4 oz	(¼ lb)
155 g	5 oz	
185 g	6 oz	
220 g	7 oz	
250 g	8 oz	(½ lb)
280 g	9 oz	
315 g	10 oz	
345 g	11 oz	
375 g	12 oz	(¾ lb)
410 g	13 oz	
440 g	14 oz	
470 g	15 oz	
500 g	16 oz	(1 lb)
750 g	24 oz	(1 ½ lb)
1 kg	32 oz	(2 lb)

QUICK CONVERSIONS

5 mm	¼ inch	
1 cm	½ inch	
2 cm	¾ inch	
2.5 cm	1 inch	
5 cm	2 inches	
6 cm	2 ½ inches	
8 cm	3 inches	
10 cm	4 inches	
12 cm	5 inches	
15 cm	6 inches	
18 cm	7 inches	
20 cm	8 inches	
23 cm	9 inches	
25 cm	10 inches	
28 cm	11 inches	
30 cm	12 inches	(1 foot)
46 cm	18 inches	
50 cm	20 inches	
61 cm	24 inches	(2 feet)
77 cm	30 inches	

NOTE: We developed the recipes in this book in Australia where the tablespoon measure is 20 ml. In many other countries the tablespoon is 15 ml. For most recipes this difference will not be noticeable.

However, for recipes using baking powder, gelatine, bicarbonate of soda, small amounts of flour and cornflour, we suggest you add an extra teaspoon for each tablespoon specified.

USING CUPS AND SPOONS
All cup and spoon measurments are level

METRIC CUP				METRIC SPOONS	
¼ cup	60 ml	2 fluid ounces		¼ teaspoon	1.25 ml
⅓ cup	80 ml	2 ½ fluid ounces		½ teaspoon	2.5 ml
½ cup	125 ml	4 fluid ounces		1 teaspoon	5 ml
1 cup	250 ml	8 fluid ounces		1 tablespoon	20 ml

OVEN TEMPERATURES

TEMPERATURES	CELSIUS (°C)	FAHRENHEIT (°F)	GAS MARK
Very slow	120	250	½
Slow	150	300	2
Moderately slow	160-180	325-350	3-4
Moderate	190-200	375-400	5-6
Moderately hot	220-230	425-450	7
Hot	250-260	475-500	8-9

INDEX

Aioli 23
Apple
    almond flan 16
    butter 17
    and chicken curry soup 8
    and chicken mulligatawny 10
    and date salad with Californian salad
        dressing 9
    and fresh fig jam 17
    and lamb curry 11
    and pear mustard 17
    and plum crumble 14
    and red cabbage 9
    spice cake 13
    strudel 13
    and wild rice with quail 12
Apricot
    banana bread 85
    chutney 53
    sauce 45

Banana
    apricot bread 85
    soufflé 85
    strawberries and peach iced summer salad 37
Beef casserole with kiwi fruit 57
Berries
    see also Blueberry; Raspberry; Strawberry
    creamy 40
    flan 41
    muffins 40
    pudding 40
Beverages
    fruit cup 33
    mango mint cooler 88
    passiona 63
    passionfruit punch 63
Biscuits
    see also Slices
    citrus ring 32
Blackforest crêpe cake 49
Blueberry
    and goat's cheese salad 36
    and raspberry flan 41
Brandied grape preserve 63
Brandy snap baskets with fruit 49
Bread, banana apricot 85
Broccoli salad with lime mayonnaise 22

Cake
    apple spice 13
    Blackforest crêpe 49
    tropical fruit 84
Californian salad dressing 9
Carrot and orange soup 20
Casserole, beef and kiwi fruit 57
Cheesecake, ginger mango 82
Cherries
    Blackforest crepe cake 49
    in brandy 53
    sauce 44
    soup 44
Chicken
    see also Spatchcocks
    lemon grass 23
    mulligatawny 10
    with plum and lychee sauce 45

salad, fruited 21
soup, curried 8
stir-fried mango, with almonds 78
Chicken livers Véronique 57
Chilled soup
    cherry 44
    curried chicken 8
    custard apple 74
    pear and lime 8
    rockmelon 68
    tangy mango and cucumber 74
    two-melon 67
    watermelon 67
Chocolate cups, peach 47
Chutney
    apricot 53
    hot mango and tomato 87
    peach 53
    tamarillo 88
Citrus
    see also Grapefruit; Lemon; Lime; Orange
    and mango salad with cream dressing 20
    ring biscuits 32
Clafoutis, ruby 46
Coeur à la crème 38
Coriander and pear salad 11
Crab with honeydew melon 67
Cranberry dressing 56
Crayfish, grilled 26
Crepe cake, Blackforest 49
Curried chicken soup 8
Curry
    fruit 70
    lamb 11
    and mango soup 74
Custard, grape and wine 62
Custard apple soup 74

Dressing 11, 21, 68
    see also Mayonnaise
    Californian 9
    cranberry 56
    cream 17
    ginger mango 77
    Italian 22
    lemon yoghurt 23
    raspberry vinaigrette 36
    sesame dill 69
Duckling breast with apricot sauce 45
Dumplings, fruit-filled 38

Feijoa and guava jelly 89
Fig
    and apple jam 17
    and passionfruit jam 62
Fish
    and fruit salad 79
    lemon sole with grapes 59
    shashlik 25
Flan
    apple almond 16
    berry 41
    fruit 70
    lemon 30
    pear, with frangipani cream 14
    plum 46
Florida salad, with walnut mayonnaise 22
Frangipani cream 14
Garlic aioli 23

Geranium sorbet 27
Ginger mango
    cheesecake 82
    dressing 77
Glacé grapefruit 30
Goat's cheese and blueberry salad 36
Grape
    and chicken livers Véronique 57
    preserve 63
    turkey and Roquefort salad with cranberry
        dressing 56
    and wine custard 62
Grapefruit
    chicken salad 21
    glacé 30
    marmalade 33
Grapes
    with grilled spatchcocks 58
    with lemon sole 59
Gremolata 24
Guava and feijoa jelly 89

Honeydew melon
    with crab 67
    and rockmelon summer soup 67
Honeyed fruits 50

Ice cream
    mango 82
    peach, with fresh peaches 51
Iced summer salad 37
Italian dressing 22

Jam
    feijoa and guava jelly 89
    fig and passionfruit 62
    fresh fig and apple 17
    grapefruit marmalade 33
    persimmon 88
    plum 52
Jelly, feijoa and guava 89

Kiwi fruit
    and beef casserole 57
    and cashew salad 56
    and mango meringue 60
    and mango sorbet 61
    sauce 60
    sorbet 83

Lamb
    curry 11
    racks with parsley mint crust 76
Lemon
    coconut slice 32
    curd 31
    and fish shashlik 25
    and garlic aioli 23
    gremolata 24
    grilled crayfish 26
    and lemongrass chicken 23
    and rose geranium sorbet 27
    sorbet 28
    soufflé, chilled 28
    tart 30
    and watercress sauce with poached
        oysters 25
    yoghurt dressing 23
Lemon grass chicken 23
Lemon sole with grapes 59

Lime
  mayonnaise 22
  and pear chilled soup 8
  rice 26
Lychee
  cocktail 74
  and plum sauce with chicken 45

Mango
  chicken with almonds, stir-fried 78
  and citrus salad with cream dressing 20
  and cucumber soup 74
  ginger cheesecake 82
  ginger dressing 77
  ice cream 82
  and kiwi fruit meringue 60
  and kiwi fruit sorbet 61
  melon and snow peas with poached scallops
    in sesame dill dressing 69
  and mild curry soup 74
  mint cooler 88
  mint sauce 76
  and prawn salad 81
  sauce 60, 87
  sorbet 83
  and tomato chutney 87
Marmalade, grapefruit 33
Mayonnaise
  aioli 23
  lime 22
Melon
  see also Honeydew melon; Rockmelon;
    Watermelon
  mango and snow peas with poached
    scallops in sesame dill dressing 69
  salad, spicy 68
  summer soup 67
Meringue, summer fruit 60
Mirepoix 12
Mousse
  passionfruit 61
  peach 50
Muffins, berry 40
Mulligatawny 10
Mustard, apple and pear 17

Orange
  and carrot soup 20
  crust pastry 30
  Florida salad, with walnut mayonnaise 22
  sorbet 28
Ossobuco alla Milanese 24
Oysters, poached, with watercress sauce 25

Passiona 63
Passionfruit
  and fig jam 62
  mousse 61
  passiona 63
  punch 63
  sauce 63
Pastry, orange crust 30
Pawpaw
  with smoked turkey 80
  sun glory pudding 80
Peach
  chocolate cups 47
  chutney 53
  and date slices 50
  ice cream with fresh peaches 51

mousse 50
and plum frozen terrine 47
poached 50
strawberries and banana iced summer
  salad 37
Pear
  and apple mustard 17
  baked surprise 15
  and coriander salad 11
  prosciutto 12
  tart with frangipani cream 14
Persimmon jam 88
Pineapple
  pizza supreme 75
  sorbet 83, 86
Pizza supreme 75
Plum
  and apple crumble 14
  butter 53
  flan 46
  jam 52
  and lychee sauce with chicken 45
  and peach frozen terrine 47
  ruby clafoutis 46
Pomegranates with veal 79
Pork
  roast with cherry sauce 44
  salad with ginger mango dressing 77
Prawn and mango salad 81
Preserve, brandied grape 63
Prosciutto, pear 12
Pudding, mixed berry 40
Punch
  mixed fruit cup 33
  passionfruit 63

Quail with wild rice and apple 12

Raspberry
  and blueberry flan 41
  coeur à la crème 38
  vinaigrette 36
Red cabbage and apple 9
Red wine sauce 58
Rice, lime 26
Rockmelon
  and honeydew melon summer soup 67
  soup 68
Rose geranium sorbet 27
Ruby clafoutis 46

Salad
  apple and date, with Californian salad
    dressing 9
  blueberry and goat's cheese 36
  broccoli, with lime mayonnaise 22
  citrus and mango, with cream dressing 17
  coriander and pear 11
  fish and fruit 79
  Florida, with walnut dressing 22
  fruited chicken 21
  iced summer 37
  kiwi and cashew 56
  mango and prawn 81
  pork, with ginger mango dressing 77
  spicy melon 68
  summer, with raspberry vinaigrette 36
  tabbouleh 17
  turkey and Roquefort, with cranberry
    dressing 56

Salad dressing see Dressing
Sauce
  see also Dressing
  apricot 45
  cherry 44
  kiwi fruit 60
  mango 60
  mango mint 76
  passionfruit 63
  red wine 58
  spicy mango 87
Scallops, poached, with melon, mango and
  snow peas in sesame dill dressing 69
Sesame dill dressing 69
Shortcake, fresh fruit 47
Slices
  lemon coconut 32
  peach and date 50
Smoked turkey with pawpaw 80
Sorbet
  kiwi fruit and mango 61
  lemon 28
  orange 28
  pineapple 86
  rose geranium 27
  tropical 83
Soufflé
  banana 85
  chilled lemon 28
Soup
  see also Chilled soup
  carrot and orange 20
  mild curry and mango 74
Spatchcocks, grilled, with grapes 58
Stir-fried mango chicken with almonds 78
Stone fruit
  see also Apricot; Cherries; Lychee; Peach;
    Plum
  brandy snap baskets 49
  honeyed 50
  shortcake 47
  with sour cream 46
Strawberry, peach and banana iced summer
  salad 37
Strudel, apple 13
Summer fruit with sour cream 46
Summer salad
  iced 37
  with raspberry vinaigrette 36
Sun glory pawpaw pudding 80

Tabbouleh 20
Tamarillo chutney 88
Tart see Flan
Terrine, peach and plum 47
Tropical fruit cake 84
Tropical sorbet 83
Turkey
  and Roquefort salad with cranberry
    dressing 56
  smoked, with pawpaw 80

Veal
  ossobuco alla Milanese 24
  with pomegranates 79
Vinaigrette, raspberry 36

Watermelon soup 67